To Alan,

Who first encouraged
me to put pen to paper.

— Harold Beator.

Foundations of
International Marketing

Steve Johnston and Harold Beaton

INTERNATIONAL THOMSON BUSINESS PRESS
I T P® An International Thomson Publishing Company

London • Bonn • Boston • Johannesburg • Madrid • Melbourne • Mexico City • New York • Paris
Singapore • Tokyo • Toronto • Albany, NY • Belmont, CA • Cincinnati, OH • Detroit, MI

Foundations of International Marketing

Copyright © 1998 Steve Johnston and Harold Beaton

First published by International Thomson Business Press

 A division of International Thomson Publishing Inc.
The ITP logo is a trademark under licence

British Library Cataloguing-in-Publication Data
A catalogue record for this book is available from the British Library

First edition 1998

Typeset in the UK by J&L Composition Ltd, Filey, North Yorkshire
Printed in the UK by The Alden Press, Oxford

ISBN 1–86152–164–2

International Thomson Business Press
Berkshire House
168–173 High Holborn
London WC1V 7AA
UK

http://www.itbp.com

Contents

Preface

We have written this book to fill a gap in the market for a textbook for university students of international marketing. We were keen to include the following topics:

- The European Union and its implications
- The marketing of services internationally
- The technical aspects of international marketing
- The importance and role of SMEs (small and medium-sized enterprises)
- Wider geographical focus of case studies, extending beyond the UK and USA

We believe that these are necessary to help the student to gain a comprehensive understanding of the subject. The world of international marketing is no longer dominated by Anglo-Saxon companies, and this is reflected in our choice of case studies which is truly international. Last but not least, a survey carried out in 1992 concluded that 99% of the companies within the European Union had fewer than 10 workers. We have therefore not concentrated on the multinationals at the expense of smaller companies.

We have striven to adhere to academic rigour and at the same time keep the style clear and simple. International marketing is a fascinating activity and although the authors have been practising and teaching it for many years, we acknowledge we still have much to learn. The international environment is changing fast and our ideas and attitudes must change with it. To learn for the future means anticipating change and thinking creatively to produce radical solutions for new problems and fresh approaches for new opportunities.

Much of this book is devoted to case studies and examples, to make the text more interesting and more instructive. We believe that successful business should drive business theory, rather than outmoded theory trying to drive the business of the future. The businesses of the future will certainly be very different from those of today.

In the past 25 years international business and international marketing have undergone changes which have been both deep and wide. The passing of the Single European Act, the collapse of the Berlin Wall, and the apparent collapse of communism in the former Soviet Union are just some examples of these changes. All of these have effects which could reverberate well into the twenty-first century, but which we cannot yet quantify. We can be sure that the changes over the next 25 years will be just as important. Any text which ignored the changes which have already taken place would be in danger of becoming mere history.

At the threshold of a new millenium, a book about international marketing needs to highlight the triple concepts of change, innovation and competition.

Our main aim in this book is to communicate the exciting, challenging and multifaceted nature of international marketing in both theory and practice.

Few business subjects offer so many different topic areas within them as does international marketing. For this reason we planned the book in such a way that the more important themes are dealt with on several different occasions. All the key concepts are defined in the first three chapters. Subsequently we examine them in greater detail. Many different strands therefore run through this book, but if you study each chapter carefully before you proceed to the next one, you will understand how these themes come together.

However, do not be discouraged if all is not clear by the end of the first few chapters. International marketing is a vast area of study and this text represents only the foundations of it, using many examples, along the way, of successful firms.

We suggest you study this book one chapter at a time, trying to master each chapter before you proceed to the next. This is because there are a number of concepts at the beginning of this book which may be totally new to you. If you take your time over the first few chapters you will make more progress later on.

Each chapter has the same structure:

1 The **topic** of the chapter with an indication of what other topics in international marketing it most closely relates to. This will help you to build up an overall picture of what international marketing is all about, and not just the individual components. The **essential learning points** of the chapter are also given.

2 The **questions** you should be able to answer by the end of the chapter. This does not mean that if you read the chapter quickly you will be able to master these questions immediately afterwards. These questions are to help you focus your mind on the different topics within a chapter. Research shows that you remember best when you learn actively. So you might take one question at a time, study it, and only proceed with the chapter when you are sure you understand that topic.

3 Each chapter contains a **body of theory**, and also **case studies** which illustrate some of that theory. Concentrate on the case studies which you personally find most interesting, and try to sort out which aspects of the case study appear in the theory of that chapter and which do not. Our analysis of each case study is not exhaustive. Remember that successful firms are the ones that make things happen, so frequently they do not do everything by the book. Instead they 'write the book', by doing things in different ways from other firms. That is often the secret of their success.

4 **Chapter review**. Using this you should be able to recall the general contents of the chapter on your second reading of it.

5 At the end there are **two sets of questions**. The first five are straightforward. They could be used for class discussion or for group work outside the classroom. You will not find all the answers to these questions in the text. Any textbook on international marketing would be incomplete if it did not emphasize the need for you to do some personal research and analysis. The second set of questions is more complex. You may feel inclined to leave these for a few weeks after you have read the chapter, and then go back to them. By then you will have a better understanding of the chapter. They have also been designed as revision questions for examinations.

The **main themes of each chapter** are summarized in a form which could be copied onto overhead projector slides for use by the lecturer or for student group work. These are given in an appendix.

Try to keep your learning active. Read only a few pages at a time. Then ask yourself one of the questions at the beginning of the chapter, at first using the book, then, when you feel confident enough, without it.

1

Some success stories from international marketing and the reasons behind them

We will start by looking at a success story in international marketing, before analysing some of the theories of international marketing and asking why this firm was a success at that time. We shall explain some of the more common terminology used in international marketing. We will analyse four factors which are of capital importance in the international marketing environment – commitment, change, innovation and competition. We will then look at another example of a firm which has succeeded for different reasons with a different type of product and in a different type of market. Finally we will examine the main reasons a firm may become involved in international marketing.

This chapter introduces some of the main themes of the international marketing environment.

❑   BY THE END OF THIS CHAPTER YOU SHOULD:

■   **Understand how and why some firms achieve success in inter-national marketing**

■   **Understand some of the main terms used in international marketing**

■   **Understand the roles of long-term commitment, change, innovation and competition in international marketing**

■   **Be aware of the main trends in the flow of world trade**

■   **Be aware of the reasons firms initially become involved in international marketing.**   ❑

Some aspects of international marketing

International marketing can be as exciting as round the world sailing. There are also other analogies with that sport. You need to master the theory, preferably before you make serious mistakes. Another similarity is that you frequently only hear of the glamorous side of both, not the hard work and long hours which are often essential to ensure success in the modern world, where competition in international marketing is becoming increasingly great. The Toshiba case study, later in this chapter, shows that often hard work is just as essential an ingredient for success as an inspired idea. Without a new concept of teamwork in product development, Toshiba's laptop computer would probably have only been a 'me too' product by the time it appeared in the shops, and much of the effort would have been wasted. As it was, Toshiba was able to obtain an important competitive advantage over its rivals.

The environment of international marketing

Four important factors, only briefly referred to by many books some years ago, now play a decisive role in international marketing and its effect on patterns of world trade. They cannot in practice be treated separately, although that is what we are attempting to do here. There is much overlap in their causes, their processes and their consequences, for both the organization and the nation.

1 Long-term planning and commitment

As we shall see in many instances throughout this book, long-term planning and commitment in an organization are just as important for success in international marketing as in a round the world trip in a small boat. Without this commitment the organization will be short in investment, or in the skilled people necessary for success, unless we understand:

- the financial implications of embarking on an international marketing policy;
- the potential dangers to firms in undertaking international marketing without realizing the risks involved;
- that without personnel with skill and experience in this area, success is impossible.

Commitment usually involves investment in people and often hardware such as appropriate premises in the target market for a marketing subsidiary.

2 Change

Before 1973 when the UK entered what was then called the European Economic Community (EEC), later to become the European Union (EU), a large percentage of its trade was carried out with European countries, but also a large percentage was carried out with Common-wealth countries. However, it became increasingly obvious to business executives that the Commonwealth countries would eventually seek new, more natural trading partners locally or regionally. In any case, some of the Commonwealth countries were arguably not ideal trading partners for the UK which was then seeking more sophisticated markets for its consumer goods, and some of the Commonwealth countries had quite low GNP (Gross National Product) per capita.

At the same time, the benefits, both political – in making wars more remote – and economic – in providing larger, more effective markets – were becoming obvious. It is therefore not surprising that the volume of trade of the UK with Western Europe has now increased to over 70%, the vast majority of this being with the European Union.

The above-mentioned change is political in its origins, and much change in the world is politically driven – as war or peace breaks out in different places.

However, much change is driven by other factors, such as social development, technological advances or change in lifestyle. Much of the Social Chapter of the Treaty of Maastricht was driven by change in social awareness, and led to legislation which guaranteed workers a minimum wage, while protecting certain groups of workers such as females and part-time workers for discrimination and unfair national legislation. The Social Chapter has had a strong influence on both the motivation and the costs of labour. All of these changes have important implications for international marketers, as we will see in Chapter 5.

Mini case study: Change   Boulogne-sur-Mer

From the mid-1970s, as well as being a seaside resort for its local French people, Boulogne enjoyed a special bonus in the form of British tourists who would arrive regularly and in large numbers, go on a shopping spree buying many forms of alcohol much cheaper than in the UK, and then return to England by ferry later on the same day. Needless to say, this represented a bonanza for both the shopkeepers and the restaurateurs of Boulogne. However, two events changed all that. The first was the Channel Tunnel project, which was some distance from Boulogne, and much nearer to its rival port of Calais. The second was the decision taken by ferry companies, in order to compete more effectively with the Channel Tunnel, to consolidate their ferry services on only one French port in order to reduce the waiting times for drivers as much as possible. Calais was chosen because it was a larger port, and because it was much nearer to the main motorways of Europe. The result was that the Boulogne tourist board had to consider how it could attract other types of tourists to Boulogne to compensate for the loss of the British day tripper.

3 Competition

At the end of the Second World War, most national economies and industries were in ruins, and only a handful of these, including the USA and the UK, could, for the time being, command a virtual monopoly in world trade. For many years following, demand in a wide range of products exceeded supply. The result, was, for at least one decade, a product-oriented world where customers were chasing after suppliers, and quality was not so important – as a customer you were grateful if you could get your hands on the product. However, with the rise of many countries to industrial status this situation gradually changed, and by the beginning of the 1980s market saturation was occurring in some industries. This led to fierce competition for customers which still continues today in many of the world's major industries, particularly steel, ship-building and the automotive industry.

An example of competition – the Spanish tourist industry

From the beginning of the 1970s British tourists flocked to Spain every summer for sun, sea, sand and the night life. Two decades later, other parts of Europe were providing fierce competition to the beaches of Spain. Portugal and Greece in particular were offering less crowded beaches at much lower prices. The Spanish Tourist Board had to review its policy and consider whether it should reposition its product in order to attract a different segment of the tourist market, which might be one offering greater profit. However, for this it would need more investment in more up-market accommodation.

4 Innovation

When a host of suppliers is chasing after a small number of customers, one of the main marketing tools that suppliers may use is innovation. Many people link this with technical innovation, and this is often the case. But there are other kinds which we will discuss later in Chapter 8. As the case study below shows, Toshiba wanted to obtain leadership in a segment of its industry's market in computers. For this it needed a totally new idea which would give new benefits to the customer – not just gimmicks. A laptop computer does just that, enabling business people to transfer work easily from home to office, and even to work on a train.

This is the case in many industries. In order to retain market share it is necessary to carry out new product development on a continuous basis. This holds true as much for services as for products as we will see in Chapter 13. Some years ago, British High Street banks all closed at 3.30 in the afternoon, and none were open on Saturdays. This was not, of course, convenient for the customers. But British banks did not then consider the customer as king. Competition has changed all that. Some have gone for innovation through offering new services, but all now offer longer banking hours and cash dispensers.

Modern customers are looking for something special

All this competition and innovation has changed another factor in the equation – the customer. Some of these are now 'shopping-happy' and looking for new 'toys' with which to impress their friends. These are the leaders, the customers who tend to buy new products first. One example of this is direct insurance, where some customers hesitated before taking

---

Case study 1: Toshiba's launch of the first laptop computer

When Atsuthi Nishida was posted to Europe in 1982 to sell the company's new laptop computers, it was a frustrating business, because there was no satisfactory software. Mr Nishida approached Lotus, makers of the world's then most popular spreadsheet, to ask them to produce their software in a form compatible with Toshiba's new machines, and they turned him down flat – the concept was too new for them. It was like the first pocket calculators – but way ahead of its time, they said. However, Mr Nishida insisted and eventually got what he wanted from Lotus.

For the first time, a Japanese company was about to gain the edge in the US-dominated world of personal computers. Toshiba had a vision that it could succeed with much smaller computers, and the dream became reality. This was not due to chance, but to the fact that the company had a long-term plan, and in addition was prepared to commit the necessary resources to the project to make it succeed.

In 1982, Toshiba had two families of portable computers. One, the T3100, was big and powerful, and used gas plasma technology. The other, the T1100, was much smaller and had some major defects.

But Toshiba's EM machine would be very different from either of these. If customers were to make the psychological leap to thinking of a computer as something truly portable, the company's engineers would have to shrink all the components of a standard PC so they would fit into an A4-sized box, but also to make a machine they could be proud of.

At the end of 1980 work had started on the project at the company's factory and research complex near Tokyo. The project design team had five leaders with teams working under them round the clock. The work was not easy because of the novel nature of the project and the time-scale envisaged.

The new product went from drawing board to the shops in less than seven months. This shows the standard of planning and commitment. The usual time in those days was at least four years. In this new project Toshiba set a precedent, as it demonstrated the parameters of the possible. However, the other Japanese computer companies, though taken by surprise by this outstanding breakthrough, soon had plans to compete with Toshiba in this market. The result was that Toshiba had a monopoly on the product for only six months. It is naturally easier to follow the leader! This is because you know it *can* be done. In addition you have a blue-print which you may follow.

Yet another innovative aspect of this product was that the company marketed it immediately worldwide. In those days it was usual for Japanese firms to try out their product first of all on their home market. However, the far-seeing Toshiba management wanted to be one step ahead, not just in Japan but throughout the world.

The rapid reaction of its competitors only served to spur Toshiba to even greater efforts. It developed eight new models within two years – a previously unheard-of feat. But it also showed, in doing this, that it is necessary to persist to maintain the initiative. Gaining a competitive advantage in the business environment of today is seldom an accident. You need to plan and commit the necessary resources to develop a new product before the competition does. This is one of the most important lessons in order to achieve success in international marketing. Toshiba, in this case study, was mainly involved in industrial or organizational marketing, that is, one business selling to another. However, many of the success factors here are the same as in consumer marketing, which is selling to the person in the street.

out motor insurance over the phone. But when they saw the savings they could make and compared notes with their friends, a revolution in insurance soon took place.

The need for further research

We have introduced a case study early in this chapter. This is because the theories of international marketing need to be closely linked to practice, and you need to be aware of the reasons for success in each specific case. Many of the case studies we use in this book are well-known firms. In order to fully understand international marketing, you will need to carry out further research during this course. More detailed knowledge of the subject, and more information about stories referred to here, can be found readily in journals and newspapers. In other cases we have chosen less well-known firms or products to illustrate the fact that as well as knowing the theories of international marketing, you need to apply them creatively in order to succeed. Business today is very competitive. It is somewhat like a multifaceted chess game. Each competitor in an industry is trying to achieve its goal, which nearly always means preventing the opposition from achieving theirs! While this is true inside each country, on the international scene the stakes are even greater, and the competition is keener. Industrial espionage is more common than you would think, and piracy is a constant problem for many owners of brands, whose imitations can often be bought very cheaply in many Far East markets.

While many of the theories of international marketing are very complex, we have all come into contact with the practical side of international marketing. In all developed countries a higher and higher percentage of products for sale in the shops, as well as services from insurance to holidays, are provided by a firm which is based in a country different from the one we live in. We all understand the reasons why we have bought those products. Usually, and statistics verify this, we buy foreign-made goods because the design or quality is superior, the product was available when our first-choice product was not, or the price was highly competitive. In many cases our choice is based on a combination of these factors. In other cases the product may not be produced at all in our country – bananas, for example, cannot be grown in most European countries.

What factors influence your choice?

Ask yourself what products you have bought recently that were manufactured in another country. Why do you think you chose those particular items? Was it because they were cheaper? Were they perhaps better designed? Or were they simply better suited than the other products to the particular use you had in mind? You will often find that it is a combination of factors that influences your choice of purchase.

Some definitions

In every new subject we study there are words and terms which need to be understood and which may have a different meaning in the context of international marketing. It is well worthwhile taking some time to study these explanations, because it will help later on in this book.

International trade

International trade is the flow of products and services from one country to another. Later we will study this in greater depth. In the meantime it will be useful to study Figure 1.1. This shows us that there are great differences in the flow of goods and services between the different trading blocks. Africa, for example, being a poor continent, sends relatively few products to other continents.

International marketing

This is the whole process which brings about the exchange of goods or services against value, which is usually in the form of money. This includes market research, advertising, promotion and after-sales activity as well as selling. International means that more than one country is involved in the transaction. International marketing therefore involves the use of many skills which are not needed to the same extent in the domestic marketing context. These include specific knowledge of extraneous markets, such as an understanding of their specific needs, their culture, language and any conditions peculiar to that market such as legal, climatic or other constraints.

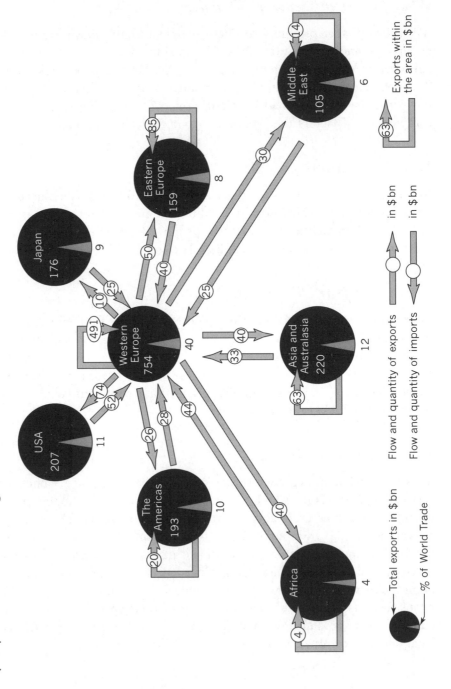

Figure 1.1 Diagram illustrating typical flows of trade between Western Europe and the rest of the world. (Adapted from 'World in Figures', *The Economist*, 1987.)

Exporting

When you come across this term in international marketing books, it is normally used to refer to the physical movement of products out of one country into another. As we shall see, this refers to only one aspect of international marketing. However, very often the media (newspapers, radio and television) use it when they really mean international marketing outwards, that is, towards other countries. Tourism can be genuinely regarded as an export, because tourists from another country are importing currency and spending it in the host country, and therefore making a positive contribution to the host country's balance of payments.

The marketing mix

This is a concept frequently used by marketers as a tool in their marketing planning and for analysing the performance of significant competitors. While it is known as the four Ps, the fourth is now more commonly referred to as 'distribution' rather than 'place', and distribution is the word we will use throughout this book.

Product

Not just the physical product, but the whole concept, as this word is used for intangibles such as services. While the perfume in a bottle is extremely important, few customers would buy a bottle of perfume which was unconventionally packaged, for example in plain brown paper. For certain goods such as cars, the after-sales service is an integral part of the product in the eyes of the customer.

Promotion

This refers to the process of informing the potential customers of the qualities of the product and persuading them to buy it. Advertising and personal selling are two common forms of promotion, but there are others, as we will see in Chapter 9.

Price

This includes various aspects of the selling price, including discounts and special offers. The price of an article often varies from one country to another. An example of this is the motor car. The price of the same model of car varies enormously even between countries of the European Union, even allowing for purchase taxes and value added tax (VAT). Generally the lowest price for most models of car is in the Netherlands and the highest in the UK.

Distribution

This involves the choice of and communications with the channel of retail distribution chosen by the organization as the most suitable. This could be specialized shops, hypermarkets or mail order. It could be different for the same product for different markets. The right decision here can be crucial to the success of a product.

Some other essential definitions

Balance of trade

This is the sum of the value of the products which a country exports, less the value of those it imports. Thus if a country imports more than it exports it will have a balance of trade deficit. It is not important if a country's balance of trade is in deficit over a short period of time, but there can be serious consequences if this deficit persists. No country, just like an individual, can prosper if its account is permanently in the red.

Global marketing

Strictly speaking, this means marketing exactly the same product at the same price and using the same promotion and channels of distribution in every market of the world. As you can imagine this is not practical, even if we consider the differing GNP per capita of various nations, and this is not the only difference. We will deal with this topic more fully elsewhere but particularly in Chapter 2.

Product adaptation

Products often need to be adapted in some way for other markets. Cars built in France for the UK market need to have their steering wheel on the right-hand side of the vehicle, for example. Product adaptation for each country would in many cases increase costs excessively so often a compromise is the answer, whereby adaptation is made only when essential.

Market segmentation

Market segmentation means dividing the market up into different segments, or groups of customers. This could be according to frequency of use of the product, customers who buy only one product, or customers who buy the whole range of products. More about this in Chapter 2.

Balance of payments

This is similar to the balance of trade but also includes invisibles such as money earned by the country from insurance, banking, tourism and other invisibles or services.

Comparative advantage

This is an economic concept rather than a marketing one. This theory states that countries tend to manufacture or produce most, what they are suited for. The Canary Islands have an ideal climate for growing a certain species of banana. It is important to understand how the comparative and competitive advantages of a country may affect its ability to maintain a balance of trade surplus.

Inward investment

This usually refers to attempts by a government to attract foreign companies to set up manufacturing subsidiaries in their country. The firms involved have a variety of motives for this. One is to choose a country with relatively cheap labour and low costs. Avoiding tariff barriers is another reason. To achieve this, firms use factories in another free trade area. By doing this, they will avoid paying tariffs on their products. The British government greatly subsidized Nissan's move to attract new jobs to an area of high unemployment.

An example of inward investment

In the mid-1970s Nissan, the Japanese car manufacturer, took the decision to open a factory in Washington, north-east England. Nissan knew there was a good labour force available with lower wages than in neighbouring countries. In addition, the Nissan management knew that by producing their cars in the United Kingdom, they would be able to avoid the quota system, which meant that the Japanese could only export small numbers of cars to certain European Union countries. Moreover, because Nissan would not have to pay tariffs on these cars, they would therefore be more competitive on the European market than they had previously been. This concept proved such a success for Nissan that they have greatly expanded their Washington factory.

Achieving results requires both commitment and resources on behalf of the government, as it does on behalf of the successful firm. Here a government is often faced with a difficult choice: to allow unemployment in a certain region to remain high, or to buy in jobs from abroad in the form of subsidies. In 1997, the British government decided to encourage the Korean firm LG to invest millions of pounds sterling in Wales in setting up a manufacturing base for microchips. The cost was high – £30,000 per job. This must be weighed against the cost of paying unemployment benefit, and also how long-term the project really is going to be.

The importance of currency stability

Strong fluctuation in the value of a country's currency is a major obstacle to successful international marketing, because it is then difficult for international buyers to predict the prices of goods from that country. A country highly reliant on one or two commodities in the world market may find that these are unexpectedly rising or falling in value, because of changes in annual crop yields or a change in mining conditions in a distant country which competes directly with it in those industries. Again, a sharp rise or fall in the value of a country's currency may greatly affect its export performance. A steady currency value is what most international marketers desire most.

Competitive advantage

Some countries, such as Japan and Germany, have over the years continued to mark up huge surpluses in their balance of trade despite the fact that their currency was gaining steadily in value against other currencies. In other words, their products were relatively more expensive. One reason for their success is that many of their firms have a strong competitive advantage over their rivals. Competitive advantage may be superior design of the product, a more user-friendly product, such as a car that needs servicing less often, or it may be that it simply fits in better with the needs of the customer. Competitive advantage is not a permanent feature of a product, and most firms spend a lot of time and effort in planning how they can improve their current products to fend off the competition. We saw in the Toshiba case study how the other firms in the industry made every effort to catch up with Toshiba's competitive advantage.

A 'me too' product

This is a product which is very much the same as many other products. It is therefore difficult to sell in international markets where the competition is usually keener than in domestic markets. A pair of jeans without a designer label is a 'me too' product.

Changes and tendencies in world development in recent times mean that if you are in niche markets or manufacturing certain types of goods you can have enormous international potential if your product is unique or has a sound competitive advantage, despite tariffs and other barriers. For this, homework is essential prior to entry operations, and field work is very often a necessary prerequisite. But we will discuss this in greater depth in Chapter 5.

The examples used throughout the course are taken from different types of country – Third World, developing, newly industrialized countries and developed – and from different types and structure of organization, product and service (see Figures 1.2 and 1.3). Students will also be

Figure 1.2 Breakdown of the world trade in goods and commodities. (Adapted from 'World in Figures', *The Economist, 1987.)*

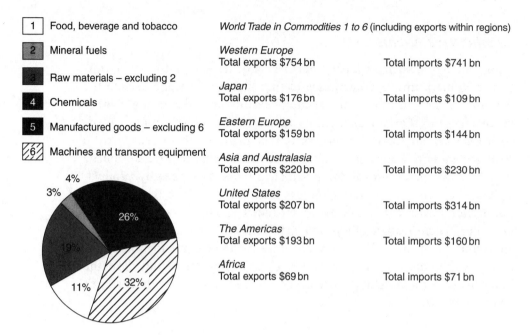

1	Food, beverage and tobacco	*World Trade in Commodities 1 to 6* (including exports within regions)
2	Mineral fuels	*Western Europe*
3	Raw materials – excluding 2	Total exports $754 bn Total imports $741 bn
4	Chemicals	*Japan*
		Total exports $176 bn Total imports $109 bn
5	Manufactured goods – excluding 6	*Eastern Europe*
6	Machines and transport equipment	Total exports $159 bn Total imports $144 bn

Western Europe
Total exports $754 bn   Total imports $741 bn

Japan
Total exports $176 bn   Total imports $109 bn

Eastern Europe
Total exports $159 bn   Total imports $144 bn

Asia and Australasia
Total exports $220 bn   Total imports $230 bn

United States
Total exports $207 bn   Total imports $314 bn

The Americas
Total exports $193 bn   Total imports $160 bn

Africa
Total exports $69 bn   Total imports $71 bn

made very much aware of the vital role of change, competition and innovation, and their effect on international marketing operations.

The success story of Swatch (see Case Study 2) is very different from others, but many success stories have some themes in common: often they are not a simple question of a bright idea linked to international marketing theory followed by implementation and bingo! – **success**. Unfortunately, international marketing is seldom as simple as that although sometimes it is, as we will see later in other case studies. More often it follows the pattern of perseverance, with success coming perhaps 20 years later, as in the case of the Japanese car manufacturer Toyota.

Toyota's first attempt at the Californian market was an almost total disaster. The Californians described their cars as built like tanks, unreliable and too small to get into. But in the face of this robust criticism Toyota, instead of giving up, learned from their 'mistakes'. Today, the

Figure 1.3 GNP per capita highlighting the contrast between rich and poor countries. (*Source*: *World Reference Atlas*, Dorling Kindersley, 1996.)

The following figures show what a contrast exists between the GNP per capita of not only the very richest and the very poorest countries, but also between countries in the same group, e.g. countries within the Organization for Economic Development and Cooperation, usually referred to as OECD countries, have quite a divergence of GNP per capita within them. GNP per capita usually gives an international marketer an idea of the spending power of the consumers in an individual country. The figures need to be treated with caution, however, for two reasons: (1) as we will discuss in greater depth later when we examine the problems of international marketing research, not all countries observe the same degree of accuracy when collecting their statistics; (2) in some countries the class structure may greatly distort the overall picture. A few millionaires within a small country may make the average consumer seem richer than he really is.

OECD countries	*GNP per capita per annum (US dollars)*
Switzerland	37,180
Japan	34,360
United States	25,860
Germany	25,580
France	23,300
United Kingdom	18,410
Australia	17,980
Emerging countries	
Malaysia	3,520
Indonesia	880
Africa	
Tanzania	90
Somalia	100
Sierra Leone	150
Nigeria	280
Latin America	
Chile	3,500
Argentina	8,060
Brazil	3,370
Bolivia	770
Asia	
India	310
China	530
Middle East	
Saudi Arabia	7,240
Qatar	14,450
Lebanon	2,107
Syria	1,218

Case study 2: A brief history of Swatch

Today Swatch is a well-known name and the Swiss watch industry is thriving. However, this was far from the state of affairs 15 years ago. Oddly enough, it was a Swiss engineer who invented the quartz concept which was to revolutionize the world watch industry and make the mechanical watch a thing of the past for most people. However, unfortunately for the Swiss watch industry, it was the Japanese who saw the potential and invested in highly automated factories. Soon the world market was flooded with Japanese watches, two brands of which are still among the world's leaders – Seiko and Citizen. They offered customers a very high standard of accuracy and reliability at a very low price, and their marketing was very good.

As a result of this competition, mainly from Japan but also from other countries in the Far East, by 1978 the Swiss watch industry, despite two centuries of world leadership, was on its knees. Nicholas Hayek was given the job of consultant to try to put Humpty Dumpty together again. Most experts thought it was a question of mission impossible. His idea of combining the two leading firms in the Swiss watch industry was regarded with scorn by experts. But often he who dares wins in the international marketing arena. Hayek had a daring plan, and it was the very boldness of this plan, as with so many successes in international marketing, that was the key to its triumph. The plan was simply to attack the Japanese in the sector where they would least expect it, namely in the cheapest sector of the market.

To succeed in this highly competitive segment of the market, Hayek needed a brand new idea, or rather a combination of brand new ideas, which worked in the long run like a charm, although not without vast investment being put into a small number of highly automated factories. The great weakness of the Swiss watch industry had been its reliance on a huge number of very small manufacturing units which led to fragmentation. What was needed, and this is what Hayek understood, was economies of scale. This is why the Swiss were in no position to compete initially with the Japanese watch industry. Hayek changed all that, despite the opposition of the old guard in the Swiss watch industry who said that putting two ailing firms together was a recipe for disaster for both of them.

What was new about the concept of Swatch? It was really a number of brilliant concepts which fitted together like a jigsaw puzzle and worked admirably well together:

- The idea of a second watch.
- Emphasis on a well-tried international marketing idea – the importance of country of origin (we will return to this theme later in the book); in this case Switzerland had a two-century-old reputation for excellent watches. 'Swatch' suggests simultaneously 'Swiss Watch' and 'Second Watch'.
- The idea of a watch as a fashion accessory.

But without the final element all would have been in vain. At that time a breakthrough had been made in plastics; hitherto plastic objects were often regarded as cheap and nasty – the colours were poor and faded easily, and the texture felt bad to the skin; but now very attractive colours were available which would not fade.

The whole marketing mix for Swatch had so many strengths:

- Product: this was new but met latent demands for customers; a latent demand is one which is not obvious.
- Price: this was eminently affordable thanks to Hayek's strategy of reducing price by economies of scale; of course, for this he needed high investment at the outset.
- Promotion: one of the most brilliant aspects of Swatch was the message: a promise of high quality at a low price; moreover, Swatch do not believe in year-on-year price increases. To illustrate the message of quality and toughness, at its launch Swatch watches were shown first of all under water, and then bounced off walls, to show just how robust they were.
- Distribution: this is where luck favoured the company; to be more exact, Jacobi, the then Chief Executive Officer of Timex, the US watch-making giant, made a classical error in international marketing. Swatch offered him the sole distribution of Swatch watches, and he turned them down. However, to be fair to him, they were presented to him then as a black and white accessory; the colours were added later and it was the idea of colours and design which makes Swatch the winner it is today.

United States, and especially California, is one of Toyota's most successful markets, and the Toyota Corolla was up until 1996 the most sold model of any car in the world. Today, Toyota has many factories in the USA.

The expansion of world trade

World trade is expanding today faster than ever before. But this expansion is neither uniform not haphazard. Many countries' imports expanded between 1977 and 1990 at approximately the same rates as other countries with a very different profile. However, the absolute differences in their participation in world trade may remain very large. By the end of this book we will understand why some nations and companies have a competitive advantage in world trade, and how some emerging nations are threatening to overtake more traditional exporting countries.

Some practitioners would argue that there is no such thing as 'international' marketing any more than there is 'international' physics. The same universal laws apply everywhere. While this may be true of physics, man has erected certain barriers between countries such as customs regulations and tariffs, while nature has provided space which must be crossed to get to the target country. Barriers, whether they are tariffs or other obstacles, require expertise to be aware of them and then to overcome them, an expertise not required in domestic marketing. In addition, the extra transport involves not only extra cost, but know-how in being able to calculate this accurately in advance. If the shipping costs of your product are exaggerated, then the contract may go to a competitor, but if they are understated, the firm will not make the profit it had anticipated, indeed it could even suffer a loss on the transaction. Such a loss could discourage the firm from further international marketing ventures.

Reasons for involvement in international marketing

Why do so many otherwise good companies shy away from entering foreign markets? One reason is the extra competitiveness which exists when marketers are no longer on their home territory. This can vary enormously depending upon the size and desirability of the market. Sometimes competitiveness has been built up over many years as in the case of the printing industry in Germany. But a hard-earned advantage can sometimes disappear quickly, as when the Japanese used new technology to overtake the German printing industry (see Porter's Competitive Advantage of Nations). So advantage can be transient, and this frequently occurs in high technology industry, where innovation can be the most important factor. In this case firms may compete with each other, mainly using technical innovations.

Certain markets such as Germany tend to attract competition from all over the world, firstly because it is a large and affluent market, with a high GNP per capita, which usually means high spending power of consumers. Secondly because it has over the past three decades, evolved a broad network of international trade fairs which attracts exhibitors as well as buyers from all the world's manufacturing nations. We will examine this topic in more detail in Chapters 9 and 14. Markets such as this tend to be highly profitable in the long term for companies with a product with a distinct competitive advantage.

One consideration which we should bear in mind is that while world trade has been increasing at an unprecedented rate over the last decade, this increase has been mainly between the affluent nations of the world. The debt of many other nations is just as important as their intrinsic poverty in natural resources as well as lack of education and training, in preventing them from participating in this increase. Nations with very low GNP per capita do of course import goods too. But these imports will be of a different nature from those of developed countries. Some of the main exports from OECD countries to Third World countries are capital goods, such as power stations or manufacturing plant. Exports from Third World countries are often of relatively low value.

Why organizations become involved in international marketing

The following are some of the conventional reasons given for a firm to enter international marketing for the first time.

- To increase the sales volume of the firm and thereby the profits.
- To increase the sales volume in order to achieve a competitive advantage in price through economies of scale. This applies mainly to certain manufacturing processes, especially but not only those where a large proportion of the work can be done by robotics or machinery. In cases where no significant cost reduction in manufacture may occur, it may be possible to bring about a substantial reduction in the price of raw materials and components by bulk buying. However, the absence of economies of scale need not be a

deterrent to smaller firms engaging in international marketing. Smaller firms may often compensate for their lack of economies of scale by their greater flexibility.

- Due to a gap in an export market which the firm has detected through its marketing research. This will mean that there is demand for the product in that market, and furthermore, it is likely that the firm may be able to ask a premium price for its products there if the niche is distinctive enough, thus returning healthy profits.

- The domestic market has entered a recession, and overseas markets are targeted as a compensation for lost sales. In such a case, a firm must be careful, when the domestic recession has ended, not to start favouring domestic customers at the expense of overseas ones. In this way they can easily lose valued customers. This depends on how the firm is structured. If the export department is perceived as a separate entity, this may lead to a tug of war for scarce products between the domestic and the overseas sides.

- To create employment. There is pressure on many governments today to reduce unemployment. In any case, any philanthropic entrepreneur may well have this as one of his or her business aims.

- To acquire prestige for firm or executive. Some executives believe they acquire prestige by being seen to be flying around the world after business. On the other hand, some products do acquire prestige and sales by being perceived as international – expensive perfumes or expensive suits, for example.

- Certain manufacturing processes are designed mainly with large-scale production in mind. If a factory in this type of industry is running at under its potential capacity two problems may arise:

  - Their costs per unit will be much higher than the competition, assuming they are using similar machines.
  - They will be missing out on the contribution factor.

So utilizing all of a factory's manufacturing capacity will reduce their unit costs and their price.

- To extend the product life cycle. A product may go out of fashion or be superseded by another one in the domestic market. However, there may still be a strong demand for that product in some overseas markets.

- The technology of the product has been overtaken in the domestic market, but there could well be a demand for the product in other markets. The Morris Minor was a well-built car which needed less maintenance and was rugged, but which went out of fashion. It was later manufactured on the Indian subcontinent where it was easier to maintain than more sophisticated cars.

- To spread the financial risks. This is more effective if the firm targets countries which are not within the same group, and are therefore likely to have different trade cycles and recessions at different times.
- The demand for the product may be seasonal – umbrellas or ice cream. By selling in overseas markets it is possible to keep production going at an even rate without piling up costly stocks.
- The firm's competitor is selling overseas thus suggesting that we should be able to succeed there, too.

It is worth your while to study these points and try to understand them, because we will be examining some of them in greater detail in further chapters. But in the meantime we should note that it is unlikely that just one of these will apply to one organization. Different ones, for example, could be valid for the same firm but for different markets, and are likely to change over time as overseas markets develop.

Chapter review

We have seen some examples of the successful practice of international marketing, by organizations which creatively used the concepts of long-term commitment, innovation, change and an awareness of competition to their advantage. Their stories are not, however, complete. These organizations need to work at maintaining their competitive advantage. We have examined some of the reasons firms become involved in inter-national marketing, and have seen that these reasons may change over time or from market to market.

Questions

Section A: Class discussion

1 List and discuss some of Toshiba's main problems.
2 Explain briefly the differences between industrial marketing and the

marketing of consumer goods. What are some of the implications of these differences?

3   What do you consider might be the main ways of promoting industrial products internationally?

4   Suggest some ways that Boulogne might attract more visitors.

5   Think of some products from other countries which you have bought recently. Analyse, in international marketing terms, the reasons you bought those particular products.

Section B: Examination revision

1   Analyse the advantages and disadvantages of launching internationally a product which is a totally new concept.

2   If the Spanish Tourist Board wishes to reposition its product (Spain as a tourist attraction), what factors would it need to consider?

3   Critically analyse Swatch's launch of its product. What alternative or complementary marketing methods could have been used?

4   Do you consider the current international marketing environment to be static or dynamic? Give your reasons, with contemporary examples.

5   Analyse how non-marketing factors influenced the success of both Toshiba laptop computers and Swatch.

References

Barclays Bank (1979) BETRO Report.

Doole, I. and Lowe, R. (1997) *International Marketing Strategy, Contemporary Readings*, International Thomson Business Press.

Porter, M.E. (1990) *Competitive Advantage of Nations*, Free Press, New York.

Planning and commitment for international marketing

2

❏   CHAPTER PREVIEW

Planning is even more important in international marketing than in most other aspects of business. Simply because it is multifaceted, it offers a wide variety of opportunities, but it also presents a large number of pitfalls for those without sufficient expertise or who have not indulged in careful planning. Planning itself is something you don't see if it is in place, as all runs smoothly. If it is not in place, financial problems or problems connected with lack of expertise in culture, languages or the technical aspects of international marketing can rapidly bring an organization to its knees. The rapidly changing nature of today's world emphasizes this need for planning.

   This topic relates to most of the key areas of international marketing, including market selection strategy, market entry strategy and the cultural impact of international marketing.

❏   BY THE END OF THIS CHAPTER YOU SHOULD:

■   Understand why long-term planning is essential for success in international marketing

- ■ Understand the foundations of international marketing planning

- ■ Understand the meaning of global marketing

- ■ Be aware of the main arguments for and against globalization

- ■ Understand why you need to understand organizational marketing in order to understand international marketing

- ■ Understand the financial implications of becoming involved in international marketing

- ■ Understand the role of channels of distribution

- ■ Understand the reasons behind the segmentation of markets. ❏

Definitions

First we will give some definitions of concepts which you may not have come across before.

SMEs: Small and medium-sized enterprises

Definitions of SMEs vary from country to country, some regarding anything with fewer than 10 employees as an SME, while in other countries the definition varies depending on whether you take turnover, number of employees or amount of capital involved. One thing, however, is clear: they are very important, and this importance is recognized in very few books on international marketing. According to one survey carried out in 1992, 99% of all the 13 million firms within the European Union have fewer than 10 employees. We therefore need to consider what international marketing techniques are used by SMEs. While Chapter 14 concentrates on SMEs, many of the techniques and marketing tools examined in this book can be used by SMEs. The area where there is most divergence of approach between SMEs and larger firms is in market entry strategy, and this subject is dealt with in depth in Chapters 6 and 7.

Multinational companies, known as MNCs or sometimes MNEs (multinational enterprises)

These are large firms which often manufacture in a number of countries, exploiting low labour and other costs. They may also establish a manufacturing plant in a free trade area in order to gain access to those markets without paying prohibitive tariffs.

Market entry strategy

This can be the use of an intermediary such as an agent or distributor, selling direct to the market through a salesforce or having a wholly owned marketing subsidiary in the market. Other options for larger firms can be takeovers or licensing arrangements, and these options are examined in Chapters 6 and 7.

Channels of distribution

These are the types of distribution used in the target market to sell to the end user/consumer. These can be hypermarkets, specialist retail stores or mail order. The choice of the appropriate channel is vital.

One important key to success in international marketing: Long-term planning

Various reports on the success factors in international marketing, such as the BETRO Report published by Barclays Bank in 1979, indicate the vital importance of long-term planning and commitment. By commitment we mean commitment of resources. Plans without the commitment of resources are meaningless. The traditional view of the development of the involvement of an organization in international marketing has been as follows:

1 Accidental exporting through orders received
2 Exploitation of a few favourable overseas markets using unmodified products
3 Planned exporting of products, usually with some modification
4 Planned international marketing operation, prioritizing markets

Case Study: King of the lollipop world

You might think that conquering the world with lollipops would be kiddies' stuff. But this case study illustrates the amount of planning needed for success in international marketing, even for a product which seems as simple as child's play.

Enrique Bernat Fontlladosa was born in Barcelona in 1924 into a family of sweet manufacturers. He worked in the family firm during the critical years of the Spanish Civil War, when ingredients for sweets were hard to come by, and improvization was the order of the day. Perhaps this factor sharpened Enrique's creative faculties and prepared him for the successes that were to come.

His first managerial post was in 1955 in charge of a sweet manufacturing company based in Oviedo, Spain. Almost at once he conceived a brilliant idea. 'Why manufacture so many different products for one market, rather than one product for many markets?', he asked himself.

His concept was based on two distinct business ideas, which he combined:

- **Economies of large scale**   Manufacturing large quantities of one product usually makes the operation much more cost-effective.
- **Spreading risks**   Where sales are spread over a large geographical area, the risk involved is less. This is because different countries usually have different business cycles, so that when one market is in depression, another is booming. Moreover, if the competition is tougher in one area, we can compensate in another, by charging higher prices there.

Next, he considered his market and who were his customers. Who were his end users and who were the buyers? In his case they were not the same. While mothers did the buying, it was children who consumed the product. It was here that Enrique harnessed his imagination to his business acumen. He noticed that mothers had a particular problem with the products. The children would get the sticky sweets on their hands and, worse still, on their clothes. So Enrique came up with the simple but effective solution – a sweet on a stick. This is now called a lollipop in English. They started off with the name 'chupa' which in Spanish conveys the idea of sucking. However, after one of their more successful TV advertisements which went 'Chupa Chups' ('suck a sweet'), the brand name turned quite naturally into 'Chupa Chups', which is now a household word in Spain and many other countries.

The new product was born in 1959, but production problems soon arose which taxed the imaginative powers even of their managing director. Special sticks with the right kind of wood had to be imported from Eastern Europe. Spain, then under General Franco, was quite isolated commercially, and Enrique had to buy another firm to solve another technical problem which had arisen. From this factory came the first machine to manufacture spherical sweets automatically, and another machine to insert the sticks into them. Without these new machines, a totally new concept, the manufacturing process would have been too labour intensive, too expensive and too slow. Production increased rapidly, but so did turnover, and soon other, more efficient, machines had to be invented to deal with a completely different scale of production – machines that turned out 80 million lollipops per year.

In 1970 Chupa Chups was selling 90% of its production inside Spain and only 10% outside it. By 1990 these figures were reversed and the firm was doing 90% of its business outside Spain. Why and how did this come about?

In 1972 the firm faced the need to make an important strategic decision. The viable Spanish market for their main product was becoming saturated, so two main options were available to them:

● To diversify into other confectionery products and try to compete with firms already strong in that field
● To search for markets abroad concentrating mainly on their very successful lollipop

Without any hesitation they decide to opt for the latter. The main implications of this were that they were concentrating on their product strengths, while at the same time spreading their financial risks.

International marketing on the grand scale

So much for the why of the question above. The how was much more complicated. They decided to open branches in countries with stable currencies, so France, the United Kingdom, Germany, the USA and Japan were among the first overseas markets for them. The first three offices set up abroad were in Bonn (Germany), London and Atlanta. Before long Chupa Chups was also manufacturing in other countries, starting with a wholly owned subsidiary, Société Bernat et Cie, in France. But Chupa Chups also used other aspects of international marketing theory to augment its income. Using a home salesforce to sell imported products in addition to one's own is a well-established international marketing idea. Chupa Chups decided to implement this theory and are now the second importer in Spain of chocolates manufactured abroad, the list including such famous names as Cadbury (UK), Ferrero (Italy) Kinder eggs, Ferrero Rocher chocolates, and 'Mon Cherie' products.

Although lollipops may seem a simple product, Chupa Chups had a broad portfolio of strengths:

- High quality, based on the use of natural raw materials
- Variety in the range of products, colours and flavours
- Long shelf life; all products are guaranteed for a storage time of two years
- Continuous new product development
- The appropriate segmentation of markets
- The brand name and familiarity of the products, which are now sold in a hundred countries
- Particular emphasis on the design of the lollipops as well as their packaging. Salvador Dali and the British company Lauder have both been involved in designing this firm's products.

5   Planned international marketing operation, including wholly owned subsidiary abroad
6   As above, but including manufacture in various markets

Of course, when we look at different enterprises, we find that few conform to this pattern of evolution. This is because, while planning plays a major role in the success of many firms in international marketing, there is often, *in addition to planning*, a network system which comes about, rather than being built up in a planned manner. An organization may acquire connections in country B through the contacts of its agent in country A. In addition, chance encounters at international exhibitions, on planes and elsewhere can lead to business being done which proves to be ongoing and not just one-off. Indeed the continuous nature of much international business is an aspect which perhaps sets it apart from domestic marketing.

We have described only some of the reasons for this firm's success. Products may come and products may go, but often a strong international business relationship between two organizations based in different countries, possibly thousands of miles apart, may last for decades. However, having said that, many successful organizations have planned their success and realized that they require not only overseas markets, but the personnel with the necessary skills to succeed there in the long run. These skills include expertise in dealing effectively with a variety of different cultures, expertise in languages, and expertise in shipping and finance. We will deal with these skills in other chapters; here it is important only to realize that these skills must be planned for. Staff with these skills must be recruited or existing staff trained in them.

Financial commitments

Financial commitments are an important consideration for any firm becoming involved in international marketing for the first time. The very act of rapid expansion could involve a firm in financial difficulties if it has not thought things through. To expand its orders greatly, a firm needs to buy a much greater quantity of raw materials. This is where a firm must calculate its cash flow in advance. If it does not, it may be obliged to pay for the raw materials in advance, but be paid for its exports only one month after the goods are delivered. If the company has not arranged credit in advance to pay for the extra raw materials, it may be faced with bankruptcy. Most manufacturing firms that go into liquidation do so because of cash flow problems (that is, they cannot pay their debts), not because of a shortage of orders. Capital will also be needed for investing in new, trained personnel for international marketing.

Customer care

It is a fact of life that within any organization, some groups and some departments have more influence than others. At one stage in the United Kingdom in the 1960s, it was the fashion to appoint accountants as managing directors of organizations. This led to catastrophic results on many occasions, because the accountant often proceeded to introduce cost savings which not only greatly curtailed the expenses of the firm, but curtailed even more its list of customers. Unfortunately, cost cutting often means a decline in customer care, and customer care or added value is increasingly where successful companies have their competitive advantage. This is even more the case in international marketing than in domestic marketing, as the former often deals in more specialized products.

This chapter pursues themes started in the preceding one. There we saw how one firm, Toshiba, achieved success, and one reason for this was its proactive approach, and obsession with planning. Long-term planning is a characteristic of many Japanese firms and one reason for what has been called the Japanese Miracle. In 1965 Japan had only 6% of world exports. By 1985 it had over 11% – no mean feat for a country with no natural resources in the form of energy.

Proactive planning

As we have already seen, Toshiba was not content to sit back, see what its competitors were up to and then follow suit. But in order to be proactive, it is necessary to have efficient and effective planning. We prefer to talk about marketing planning rather than marketing plans. Maybe this is because in the 1970s there was a lot of lip service paid to marketing plans by directors. But the plans, once drawn up, would gather dust in someone's drawer for the next 12 months and were therefore of no practical value. Many Western organizations lacked the application of this long-term planning used by the Japanese. This led a Japanese wit to describe US planning as 'Ready, fire, aim'. A good example of the Japanese attitude to planning is to be found in a conversation with Konosuku Matsushita, the founder and President of the Matusiti Electric Company, one of the most successful companies in the world in a very competitive industry:

'How long are your long-term goals?'
'Two hundred and fifty years.'
'What do you need to carry them out?'
'Patience.'

Marketing planning

Marketing planning is a process, and an ongoing one at that. Plans must be continually monitored, as changes in the environment may be very abrupt and unexpected. If these changes are not noted immediately, large sums of money can be lost. Plans are often drawn up on certain assumptions. One of these might be, as in the case of UK international marketers in the late 1990s, that their currency will remain low in value, if not actually undervalued. The assumption that the currency will stay that way indefinitely can lead to an organization falling into the trap of considering its competitive advantage as one of everlasting price advantage. The problem with this strategy is that frequently it is a non-sustainable advantage, because it often relies on factors over which the organization has no control, such as the price of raw materials or the value of a country's currency compared with that of other countries. This means that when the price of that raw material rises, or the currency is revalued, the competitive advantage is lost at a stroke.

Example

During the 1970s, 1980s and early 1990s, the pound sterling was continually in decline *vis-à-vis* the Deutschmark and most other currencies. The result was that many British firms built their international marketing planning around this concept. When in late 1996 the situation suddenly changed, and the pound sterling was effectively revalued by about 20%, many British organizations were wrong-footed. Their planning was based on the assumption that sterling would fall for ever. But nothing is for ever, and that is why contingency plans are essential in international marketing.

Flexibility in planning

If fashion or the weather changes and consumers suddenly stop buying a particular item of clothing, stockists must be aware at once of the fall in sales and be prepared, if necessary, to cut back production on that article immediately, before it is too late. Otherwise large stocks will be piled up which may have to be sold off at a large discount, particularly if they are fashion or seasonable products. This year's computer games for Christmas will probably be old hat by next Christmas. This will eat into the firm's profits for the quarter. For that reason, successful firms monitor their sales on a daily basis, so that they may act quickly to avoid an over-stocking situation. Flexibility and rapid reaction are called for when such situations arise.

Figure 2.1 shows what are recognized as the essential stages in marketing planning, but because they are nearly all interactive processes they cannot be easily explained in linear format. See Figure 2.1.

Corporate objectives will include determining what business we are in now, and what business we will be in in five and ten years from now. This is not as easy as it may seem. The secret is to stand back and look at our product from the customer's point of view. We need to know a lot about the customer and his or her perception and use of our product. It is an unwarranted assumption to believe it will succeed indefinitely because it is just marginally more satisfactory than the competition, because if the competition brings out something fractionally better, our market share could decline rapidly.

The long-term future of a business depends today on the ability of its managers to determine what business it is really in. Many years ago the United States Railways decided they were in the railway business and that is why the railways have undergone a serious decline in that country. If they had realized they were in the transportation business, the name of the world's largest airline today might well be The Pacific Atlantic Railway, which could include car hire, parking lots and many other aspects of the personal transport business. Allocation of resources will be, like many aspects of our planning, on a rolling basis, that is, subject to modification as circumstances change or we achieve our targets.

Forecasting is obviously very important in international marketing. We will always want to know what our customers will be wanting tomorrow. We will deal with forecasting in Chapter 3, along with market research.

Global marketing

It would appear at first sight that nothing could be better than global marketing. It seems to offer advantages in different aspects of the marketing mix.

Figure 2.1 The corporate planning process

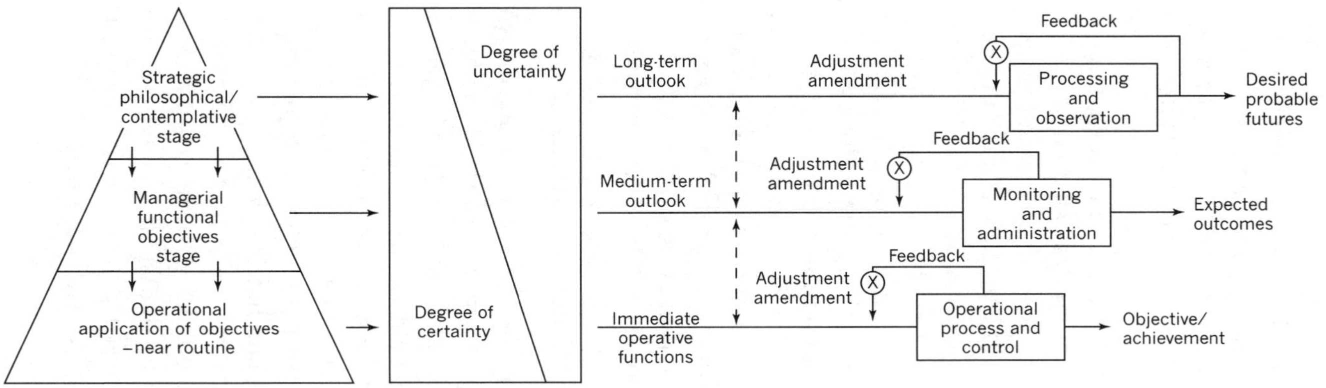

- **Product** With many types of production process, making one single product for every customer offers economies of scale, and therefore lower costs per unit. In some cases, if the raw materials needed to manufacture all the products of a range are identical, substantial discounts can be obtained on the raw materials.
- **Promotion** If we can use the same promotion material, e.g. TV advertisements, simply translated into different languages, we can greatly save on the promotion costs we would incur if we had different advertisements for each market.
- **Price** It is difficult to argue for the same price for each market, in view of the extraordinary gap in the GNP per capita between different countries. However, it could be argued that certain up-market goods, marketed mainly to OECD countries, could be sold at the same price in each country. However, despite the relative homogeneity of the European Union, the price of the same new car varies enormously from one country to another, the UK being the most expensive market for cars and the Netherlands the cheapest.
- **Distribution** An identical product being sold to different but similar markets may very well produce a steeper learning curve. That is to say, we will learn lessons from the channels of distribution we use in one market which may be transferred to give us an advantage in another, similar market.

Unfortunately there are major problems with globalization in practice for very many products. In a world of command economies where governments decide what is manufactured, globalization would present few problems. We would all drive the same grey cars and go around in the same grey suits. However, at the end of the twentieth century, consumers live in market economies, and wish to assert their personality. One of the ways they do this is by deliberately buying something that is different from the goods purchased by neighbours and friends. Who does not get a kick out of buying a car which is different from any other one in their street? It does not have to be new or expensive. It does have to be different. How do you feel if you go to a formal function, and someone else is wearing exactly the same dress as you?

Figure 2.2 shows the consumer's environment.

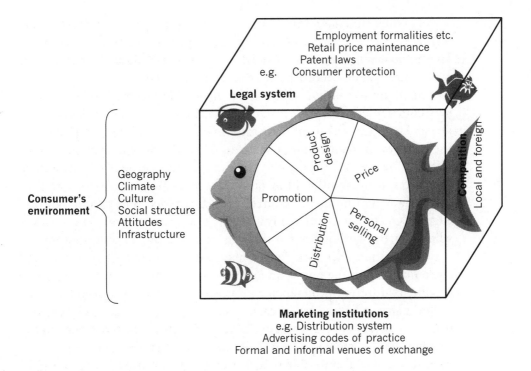

Figure 2.2 Adaptation of Majaro's ecology model. (*Source*: Majaro, S. *International Market Profile Analysis*, revised edn, Routledge, 1982).

Market segmentation

What we have just expressed in lay terms illustrates the marketing adage that the customer is king. This means that the marketer needs to anticipate the customer's needs and wants and completely satisfy them at a reasonable price in most cases. However, needless to say, things are never quite as simple as that. But let us stop for one moment and analyse the situation. At one end of the scale we have the totally customized article, such as a tailored suit or a Rolls Royce car. The latter is something that only the seriously rich can afford, even in the most affluent countries. Depending on the cost of labour available, everyone will not necessarily be able to afford a tailored suit. At the other end of the scale we have the universal suit, same colour, same design, possibly same size for everyone. This suit will be very cheap, but will probably please no one.

The compromise that marketing experts have come up with is market segmentation and targeting. Market segmentation means carrying out market research on our customers and seeing what groups we can usefully divide them into, in order to satisfy their needs and, at the same time, make our business more profitable. This may be by dividing up our customers by use of our product, by disposable income, by lifestyle, or by frequency of use of our product. These are just some of the possibilities. One of the secrets of successful marketing is thinking out new and useful ways of segmenting a market. If we divide our customers into different segments by income, we can produce products at different prices to suit these different incomes. In successful international marketing, imagination needs to be linked with theoretical and product knowledge to create competitive advantage. Finding segments of the market which our competitor has not thought of is one way of achieving this.

Segmentation therefore represents a compromise between complete customization on the one hand and one product for all on the other. By producing different products for groups of customers with similar tastes rather than a different one for each customer, we can reduce our costs and make our price more competitive while still attracting those customers. Furthermore, customers in the same segment often read the same literature, so we may also be able to target that segment in our advertising.

Products which are of a functional nature may be accepted globally, especially if they are cheap enough for everyone to afford and are of standard application. Nails, wood screws and most simple wood-working instruments come into this category. Unfortunately, not all objects which at first sight are of a functional nature can be marketed in identical form in every market. Telephones and electric kettles are two cases in point. Although these can be regarded as being functional, style and fashion now play an important role in the design of these, and people want and demand different colours and designs.

Organizational marketing

You need to have a basic understanding of organizational or business-to-business marketing to fully appreciate international marketing. This is mainly because very many SMEs need to use the tools of organizational marketing in their international marketing operations. These firms are not large enough to invest capital in advertising to their end users in overseas markets in general, although they may very well do this in the case of one or two markets with particularly high potential.

They will, however, be deeply engaged with intermediaries in many markets. These intermediaries may be manufacturers to which they market components or raw materials, or wholesalers to which they market products which the wholesalers will then sell on to retailers.

Table 2.1 lists some useful differences between consumer marketing

Table 2.1 Differences between consumer marketing and organizational marketing

Consumer marketing	Organizational marketing
Customer spends money	Customer invests money
Customer responsible to self	Customer responsible to organization
Buying decision independent	Customer decision dictated by rules
Customer has amateur status	Customer highly trained professional
Customer often lacks experience of product	Customer has expertise in use of product
Market has one level of customer	Market has more than one level of customer
Marketing opportunities exist all the time	There are only windows of opportunity
Buying decision taken by one person	Buying decision often taken by team
Product often standard	Product often customized
Purchases often 'one off'	Long-term relationships the norm
Promotion by advertising	Personal selling a key factor
Reputation of supplier not always important	Reputation of supplier always important
Salesperson has general background	Salesperson has specialized background

and organizational marketing, which you need to understand. We have analysed some of these. You can examine some of the others and try to understand the reasons for these differences.

When you as an individual go out shopping, you usually spend what you can afford. You are usually making value judgements as you go along, and you can sometimes indulge your whims, do some impulse buying of things you don't really need. However, professional buyers will normally have specific guidelines and more often than not specifications and performance of the products which they are authorized to buy for their organization, and the price range they may pay for them. If they are purchasing components for a washing machine, with a life expectancy of 10 years, then that is the kind of specification they will receive for the components. To have some components designed to last for, say, 20 years is going to have a serious impact, when all is added up, on the selling price of the washing machine. While quality and reliability are very important factors for the person buying a washing machine, they are not easily detectable in the shop. On the other hand, price is. Therefore, while branding plays an important role in the decision to buy a washing machine, so too does price. The price tag on the washing machine in the shop influences the price the professional buyer can pay for the components in that machine.

Matching quality

One of the authors once made an overseas business trip to a particular market, during which he sold very few components for washing machines. This was because the quality and price of the components he was selling were higher than the buyers were authorized to pay. The policy of the author's firm was to manufacture only the best. There was no way of finding out in advance, as we will see later in the chapter on market research (Chapter 5), that this was the case. Manufacturing low quality products was not possible because the firm would have had to change their whole manufacturing process, thus increasing the cost of low quality components to above that of their high quality products. This is often the case with short runs of production. In any case, other firms specialized in low quality components, and the author's firm could not compete with them on price. It is therefore important to match the product to its use or to its customer. For this reason, certain clothing manufacturers make garments of different levels of quality for different chains of retail outlets.

For more valuable pieces of equipment or raw materials ordered in bulk, it is usual for the buying decision to be taken by the buying team, which might consist of, for a machine, the production director, chief designer, chief engineer and managing director. Who has the most say in the purchase will usually depend on the politics of the organization and how the 'teams' line up. Finding out which members of the team have more clout is a difficult task for the salesperson, but one which he or she must attempt nevertheless. There is no point in a salesperson spending hours with the chief designer, when it turns out that no one respects his or her opinion.

The professional buyer

The professional buyer may well know more about the application of the product than the salesperson. This is because the latter will not have access to confidential information about the machine in which the component will be used. However, once two companies have been working together for some time, they often go in for informal joint ventures in the development of products. This will involve a high degree of confidentiality on both sides as regards releasing this information to third parties. It is quite common for a relationship like this to last for decades.

This kind of cooperation takes place between firms of all sizes from the smallest to the largest. Boeing is an excellent example of organizational marketing. While it sells its planes directly to airlines, it and its direct customers need to be aware of the needs and expectations of the end users, i.e. airline passengers, both now and in the future. Organizations are taking their customers more seriously as competition stiffens. In no industry is the competition greater than in the aircraft industry. The story of Boeing and its revolutionary attitude to designing the 777 is described in the case study overleaf.

Often the buyer is as dependent on the supplier as the supplier is on the buyer. If, for example, the supplier's factory burned down overnight, it would probably be impossible to replace these components in time to prevent the production line grinding to a halt. If one component for a machine is missing, it cannot simply be 'bolted on' at the end of the production line. The whole line must stop. Such an event would mean great loss of money and possibly customers as well. There are therefore

Mini case study: Working closely with customers
The Boeing 777 project

This is your customer speaking: Boeing made close contact with airlines in the development of its 777. By Michael Skapinker

On a grey and blustery day in Seattle last month, a new Boeing 777 took off from the local airfield to the cheers of the company's employees. Tomorrow, the aircraft, the US manufacturer's first new model in 13 years, makes it maiden commercial flight from London to Washington DC in the colours of United Airlines.

Mr Frank Shrontz, Boeing's chairman, says this will be the last passenger aircraft model launched by any manufacturer this century. On it rests Boeing's hopes of remaining the world's leading aircraft maker and of resisting the challenge of Airbus Industrie, its increasingly confident European competitor.

Boeing's executives say building the twin-engine aircraft, which carries up to 400 passengers, changed the way the company operated, breaking down barriers between its specialists, introducing new technology and making closer contact with customers.

Mr Philip Condit, who headed the 777 project until becoming Boeing's president in 1992, says: 'We made a whole bunch of evolutionary changes that had a revolutionary result. It's a turning point.'

The new aircraft, which sells for $ 120m (£ 75m) before discounts, was manufactured against a background of some of the worst market conditions the industry has seen. When Boeing decided to build the aircraft in 1990 it employed 161,000 people and recorded annual net earnings of $ 1.39bn. By the end of 1994, staff numbers were down to 117,000 and net earnings were Dollars 856m.

A few days after Boeing workers cheered the 777's take-off, they heard that Boeing job losses this year would be 12,000, rather than the 7,000 announced earlier in the year – although about half of those leaving will be taking voluntary early retirement.

Last year provided Boeing with a shock when Airbus recorded more orders than it did – the first time Boeing had been deprived of the top slot since the advent of the jet age. Boeing executives play down the significance of Airbus's achievements, saying it is deliveries which count.

Nevertheless, the shadow of Airbus has hung over the entire 777 project, on which analysts estimate Boeing spent $ 5bn. Mr Gordon McKinzie, the 777 programme manager at United, describes how his company openly played Boeing and Airbus off against each other in its bid to get a better deal and a better aircraft.

Towards the end of the 1980s, United, the world's largest airline, realized that it would need a replacement for its McDonnell Douglas DC-10 fleet, which would be 25 years old in 1996. In October 1990, the airline invited Boeing and Airbus, as well as McDonnell Douglas, to Chicago to present their arguments for re-equipping the United fleet.

United also invited the world's three leading aircraft engine makers, General Electric and Pratt & Whitney of the US and Rolls-Royce of the UK, to say why they should be allowed to power whatever aircraft was chosen. United called the six companies in one at a time to put their arguments over 70 hours. United had to choose between Boeing's proposed 777, the Airbus A330 and A340 and the McDonnell Douglas MD-11.

United was impressed by Airbus's 'fly-by-wire' technology, which allows the wing and tail surfaces to be controlled electrically rather than mechanically.

United decided, however, that the 777, powered by Pratt & Whitney engines, seemed the better aircraft. But the airline told Boeing that the aircraft would have to be designed and made differently from the manufacturer's previous models.

First, United said the 777 – bigger than the 767 but smaller than the 747 – would have to work properly from the day it was delivered. United did not want a repeat of its experience with the Boeing 747-400 when it, and other airlines, had to sort out early faults.

Mr McKinzie says: 'What we had in mind was orchestrating a departure from our past practice of ordering an airplane, waiting five years, then giving Boeing a final payment and flying away hoping everything aboard was as we expected.'

Second, United would help design the 777 from the beginning. Mr McKinzie says: 'We moved right into Boeing. We virtually infiltrated the Boeing process.'

Boeing decided to go further, inviting eight airlines to help it design the aircraft. They were United, American Airlines, Delta Air Lines, British Airways, Cathay Pacific, Qantas, Japan Airlines and All Nippon Airways. Three Japanese companies, Mitsubishi Heavy Industries, Kawasaki Heavy Industries and Fuji Heavy Industries, made 20 per cent of the airframe. The airlines and Boeing decided the aircraft would have fly-by-wire technology. It was designed entirely on computer, so that no mock-up had to be built.

Mini case study: Working closely with customers
The Boeing 777 project (continued)

The involvement of the airlines saved Boeing from several errors. United told Boeing that the level of the 777's fuelling panels meant the aircraft would need different fuelling trucks from those used for the 747. Boeing agreed to change the position of the fuelling panels so that the same trucks could be used for both models. United said it did not want silver plated wiring in the fuel tanks because past experience had shown that this corroded. Nickel plated wiring was used instead.

Before the 777 was completed, it had attracted 144 firm orders and 99 options. United was the largest customer with 34 orders and 34 options. Boeing claims that since work on the 777 started in 1990, the aircraft has taken a clear sales lead over the A330 and A340 and the MD-11.

Airbus concedes that the 777 has outsold the A330 and A340 since 1990, although the two companies disagree on how big a lead Boeing has. Airbus scoffs, however, at Boeing's claims that it has broken new ground in the design of the 777. Airbus says its A320 aircraft, which entered service seven years ago, was 90 per cent computer-designed. The A340, which went into service in 1993, was completely computer-designed.

Airbus also asks why Boeing should regard listening to its customers as such a feat. This is a question which manufacturers in many industries might repeat. Mr McKinzie says: 'At no time did Boeing turn us away or ignore us.' Why should the leading customer of a $ 5bn project even raise the possibility of being ignored.

Mr Gerald Greenwald, United's chairman, says the tradition of the aircraft industry is largely to blame. He says: 'Historically, airplanes have been designed by engineers for engineers and the engineers have been left to determine what's good for everyone else.'

Mr Condit says that while other sectors, such as motor manufacturers, were being forced to listen to their customers, many in the aircraft industry thought of themselves as a special case. 'There's a temptation to say: "Airplanes are different. We have a product that leaves the ground."' Mr Shrontz says he is confident Boeing can maintain a worldwide market share of 60 per cent to 65 per cent in spite of the progress Airbus has made. The challenge now will be to begin earning a return on the large investment in the 777. The orders accumulated since 1990 dried up last year, when the aircraft did not attract any new buyers. Of the eight airlines which helped design the 777, three – American, Delta and Quantas – have not ordered any. However, Boeing says airlines will buy more than 15,000 aircraft over the next 20 years. Mr Nicholas Heymann, an analyst at NatWest Securities in New York, believes the 777 is poised to gain several orders. He says Boeing's ability to produce a new aircraft with fewer people has made him optimistic about its future. 'Boeing's ability to remain competitive is not going to be challenged,' he says.

Source: *Financial Times*, 6 June 1995

The sequel to this story is that in 1997, two years later, Boeing and McDonnell Douglas sought to merge in what would have been the largest merger ever in the world aircraft industry. An ideal merger in many ways, it combined Boeing's expertise in civil aircraft with Mcdonnell's expertise in engine manufacture and military aircraft. The aircraft industry has been, as far as Europe is concerned, an international one for many years, with Germany, the UK, France, Italy and Spain often forming a consortium to produce one new fighter aircraft between them, in addition to Airbus's international operations in the civil aircraft field.

often penalty clauses for suppliers who do not deliver components on time.

In organizational marketing, when firms work together the personnel from the different firms get to know each other and form bonds, and this greatly facilitates effective communications between them. Effective communications are essential in international marketing, and we will examine these in the next chapter.

One basic difference between organizational marketing and consumer marketing is that the former has frequently two distinct but interrelated levels of customer to cater for. One is the company to which you market directly, be it wholesaler, manufacturer or assembler, the other is the end user, or person or organization which consumes the end product. The demand in organizational marketing is a derived one, that is to say it comes first and foremost from the end user. So if the demand at level one (end user) declines then so will the demand at level two (direct customer). If the demand for pullovers falls in the High Street there will be less demand for capacity in the textile firm knitting those garments and in the fibre firm spinning the thread.

The organization involved in organizational marketing must therefore keep in close touch with its two levels of customers. Where the organization is a larger one marketing to a smaller one, it needs to carry out some research into the needs and wants of the end user. This is the case with fibre manufacturers, the main thrust of whose research is with the public, to ascertain which fibres the manufacturer is developing are acceptable to them; for example, are they soft enough for their skin, do they like the look of them? These are not questions that can be decided inside a laboratory.

Chapter review

In this chapter we have examined the importance of long-term planning and commitment to international marketing, and we will see further examples of this in other chapters. We have seen how mass production and customization led to the compromise of segmentation which not only applies within markets but also between markets. Organizational marketing is an important concept internationally.

Questions

Section A: Class discussion

1 Take a well-known branded product which you have bought at least once, and which is currently marketed in a number of countries. Discuss whether this product needs adaptation for different markets.
2 List three differences between consumer marketing and organizational marketing.
3 What are the advantages of branding?
4 Why is international marketing planning more important today than 30 years ago?
5 What are the main problems of marketing a 'me too' product internationally?

Section B: Examination revision

1 'As the world becomes smaller, globalization of markets will become more and more complete.' Discuss, with examples.

2 'Globalization is completely against the spirit of international marketing, and ignores customers' wishes.' Discuss.
3 What are the advantages of branding?
4 Do you think that branding in international marketing will increase or decrease over the next few decades? Give your reasons.
5 Analyse the benefits of segmentation in international marketing.

References

Chisnall, P.M. (1989) *Strategical Industrial Marketing*, Prentice-Hall.

Majaro, S. (1982) *International Marketing – A Strategic Approach to World Markets*, revised edn, Allen & Unwin (Reprinted by Routledge, 1993).

3

Communications with the market and the role of negotiations in international marketing

❏ CHAPTER PREVIEW

Effective and efficient communications with overseas markets are a prerequisite for success. These depend often on organizational culture and teamwork rather than individual virtuosity. Negotiations in international marketing are often quite different from domestic marketing.

Both topics relate closely to long-term planning of the organization and its training of personnel.

❏ BY THE END OF THIS CHAPTER YOU SHOULD:

- Understand the importance of market selection
- Understand the meaning and significance of commercial com-
- petence and technical competence

- Be aware of the importance of teamwork in international marketing
- Be aware of the role of negotiations in international marketing
- Be aware of the main reasons for failure in international marketing.   ❏

Some more definitions

OECD

This stands for Organization for Economic Cooperation and Development and is often a shorthand used to describe the 40 or so most industrialized countries in the world. As a rule they also tend to be the wealthiest in terms of GNP per capita, so they present better opportunities for the marketing of up-market consumer goods, as well as better opportunities for industrial goods.

Country of origin effect

This varies to a considerable extent from one country to another. However, in general in OECD countries most consumers will associate Germany and Japan with excellence in cars while France is linked with female fashion and perfume, and Italy with fashion.

Piracy

This phenomenon is very common in many countries of the Far East, where Rolex watches and Levi jeans are on sale at a fraction of the normal price. This trade is worth many millions of pounds per year and it is very difficult to stamp out, particularly in videos, as it is often perpetrated by very small fly-by-night companies which are very difficult to trace.

Introduction

To achieve success in international marketing a firm needs to be concerned not only with the overall strategy or planning aspects of it but also with the tactical and concrete requirements essential to the successful implementation of any plan. One of the most important considerations in international marketing is communications between the organization and its international markets.

Concentration on key market selection strategy

Research shows – Connell's findings and those of the BETRO report – that one of the problems created for themselves by many SMEs involved in international marketing is that they often try to enter too many markets simultaneously. This leaves their scant resources overstretched. Among the weaknesses and deficiencies attributed to this dilution of effort over too many overseas markets are:

- Lack of market-specific skills
- A mismatch between product and market needs
- Insufficient after-sales service
- Inadequate monitoring of markets
- Inadequate market research.

It is easy to understand that a number if not all of the above stem from inadequacy of funds, i.e. lack of long-term commitment.

Larger firms often focus on a greater number of markets, but because of their greater resources are less likely to overstretch themselves. However, we will examine this subject in greater depth in Chapter 5.

Communications with overseas markets

Important factors with regard to communications with the overseas market include executives' visits to the market, promotion in the market, the use of foreign languages by the organization, and its commercial and technical competence. Most reports, Tookey for example, find that visits to the market and working closely with agent and distributor are crucial factors for success.

Barclay's Bank Report stresses the importance of market research and the need for the use of foreign languages by the international marketing department. Lack of knowledge of the local language can frequently mean that the principal is totally reliant on the agent or other intermediary for market information and direct contact with the end user, which constitutes a major marketing weakness. Moreover, it is difficult if not impossible to cultivate a relationship of trust with the buyer if one does not speak his or her language, and trust is the basis of international marketing and purchasing. It also helps business relationships if the customer and supplier can converse socially.

With regard to business relationships, Turnbull and Cunningham's report examined the following aspects of buyers' attitudes:

- We like dealing with them
- Business is based on mutual trust
- Easy to cooperate with
- Understands the buyer's problems
- Understands how foreign firms operate
- Easy to make friends with
- Cultural differences are not a problem
- Language differences are not a problem

Many of the above factors, while at first sight highly subjective, are also highly relevant to the effectiveness of the buyer. Consider the first example. A buyer dealing with customers on a price or purely commercial basis alone is going to suffer from severe stress if he or she cannot communicate effectively with his or her counterpart. The salesperson represents not only the product but also the firm. So unless he or she likes dealing with his or her counterpart from the other firm, communications are going to be more difficult.

The importance of commercial and technical competence in effective communications with an overseas market

Commercial competence
This consists of rapid delivery, punctual delivery, integrated delivery holding local stocks where necessary, spare parts and service and the handling of complaints. Some industries need a relatively flexible schedule, so a firm which can deliver quickly on receipt of an order will

gain many brownie points. With other industries punctual delivery, i.e. keeping to your promised date, is much more important than being able to provide a rapid delivery. However, integrated delivery is what most buyers today are looking for. This means that they will give an approximate date for an order but this date is likely to change with the changing demands of the customer's customers. Two important implications of this for the buying firm are the cash flow implications – the firm will not be paying for stocks of components or raw materials it is holding but not using, and the storage implications – they will not require nearly as much room for storage of stocks of raw materials. Both of these factors have become much more important in recent years as firms have striven to reduce costs and the fashionable 'just in time' philosophy of Japanese firms has spread to many others.

Technical competence

This consists of new technology, joint product development, product adaptation, conforming to international or free trade association (FTA) standards, having consistent quality of product and providing the appropriate technical information both about the product and for the specific market. New products are constantly being developed, and any firm which does not do this is likely to find its sales falling rapidly as it is overtaken by other, more innovative, companies. Joint product development which used to be practised by mainly the larger companies – an example is Boeing from Chapter 2 – is now practised by companies of all sizes, while the decision to adapt the product is often one of the first taken by the firm when deciding to enter overseas markets. Which standards to aspire to is not always an easy question to answer. Quite often the standard may depend more on the culture of the particular market than the standards of the FTA. In other words, what standards do the retailers in that country demand?

A reputation for commercial and technical competence is hard won and easily lost, and with increasing internationalization of companies, reputation can spread quickly across international frontiers.

The use of foreign languages in communications

Many reports on international marketing mention this area, but it seems that little changes here and that many Western European countries lose a lot of business because of their reluctance to teach their executives foreign languages. The exceptions – the Swedes, Dutch and Danes – reap their rewards in extra overseas sales. Figure 3.1 shows the communications model for international business.

Another aspect of international marketing whose importance is often not reflected in domestic marketing is negotiations. Negotiations often assume a major role in international marketing, so it is important to examine them briefly.

Figure 3.1 The communications model for international business

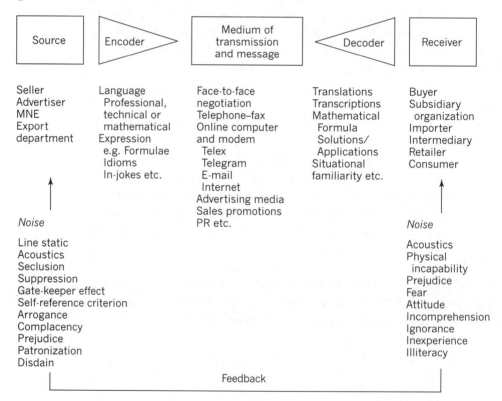

Negotiations

All ongoing international business and marketing activities include an agreement between parties, whether it is an allocation of exclusive territory, a more modest distributor agreement or even permission to use the shelf space of a local retailer. In fact, many of the different situations where parties meet and discuss ways of arriving at a situation which provides mutual benefit, require give and take, or negotiation.

In these situations each party wishes to optimize their assets and yield the minimum and will therefore to some degree avoid exposing all their concessions. This is normal in most societies, but cultural factors entering into the process may upset the equilibrium, unless there is a mutual understanding of each other's culture. It is this difference between cultures that often makes negotiations internationally different from the domestic scene.

In view of the various components and cultural orientations, which we will examine in greater depth in the next chapter, it is not surprising that difficulties may arise in the attitudes and viewpoints of the parties, which might lead to tension, exasperation and even the breakdown of negotiations. The time orientation would be a case in point. Many Western managers are imbued with the attitude of 'time is money', and will wish to show their efficiency by concluding the deal in record time. However, other cultures feel otherwise, and seek to use the negotiation process as a social event which is not to be hurried. The insistence on a quick conclusion will be seen as a breach of good taste and even possibly an admission of some form of underhand deal to the other party's disadvantage.

The writer was once informed of the viewpoint of a Middle Eastern market trader who said he felt disappointment and resentment at Western purchasers who did not haggle over the prices asked by him, thus depriving him of part of his job satisfaction.

Another important cultural norm is the distance people wish to stand from their negotiating partner. Certain cultures, including many Middle Eastern ones, feel that standing very close to another person indicates trust and esteem while persons from another culture may find this offensive or distasteful, and seek to keep a greater physical distance between themselves and their negotiating partners. We can easily imagine the confusion which such unconscious attitudes can bring about, when not understood.

The desire to please and the avoidance of refusal dominates Far Eastern culture, so that a flat refusal is not issued, but a qualified acceptance is given instead. Chinese and Japanese negotiators appreciate this, but Western managers may not be able to receive the subtle clues given out by this process, and may assume they have reached agreement, when this is not in fact the case.

The need for negotiators to be of equal status is of paramount importance in some cultures, such as Japan, and a combined negotiating team of mixed ranking or seniority may upset the feelings of the other party, who may have a strict hierarchical attitude and deliberately field their top management team for the occasion.

Need to be prepared

Negotiations in international marketing are often very different from those in domestic marketing and managers need to be fully acquainted, not only with the different cultural differences in general as examined in Chapter 4, but also with the very different attitudes to negotiations.

Main reasons for failure in international marketing

It is useful to know why firms fail in international marketing. The following list is a combination from European and US sources:

- Failure to obtain expert advice and develop an international marketing plan before becoming involved in overseas markets.
- Insufficient commitment by top management to overcome initial difficulties and financial requirements of international marketing.
- Chasing orders round the world, instead of establishing a basis for profitable business and orderly growth.
- Neglecting overseas markets when there is a domestic boom.
- Failure to treat overseas customers on the same footing as domestic ones.
- Unwillingness to modify products for overseas markets.
- Failure to prepare carefully sales and technical literature in foreign languages and with a foreign culture in view (customers in different markets often expect quite different facts from a sales or technical brochure).

- Failure to train staff.
- Failure to cultivate licences and joint ventures.

Chapter review

This chapter has focused on important issues in international marketing which need to be understood and where study and practice are needed. Market selection, communications with the target market and understanding international negotiating techniques are also necessary.

Questions

Section A: Class discussion

1 What is the significance of communications with a market internationally for SMEs?
2 List the aspects of commercial competence and discuss the importance of one of them.
3 List the aspects of technical competence and examine the significance of one of them.
4 Describe briefly the aims of the negotiation process.
5 Give examples of problems which can arise in negotiations between different cultures.

Section B: Examination revision

1 Examine why the area of communications with the market plays so important a role in international marketing strategy.
2 Which do you think is more important for communications with the market, commercial competence or technical competence? State your reasons.
3 Discuss some reasons for the potential different approach to communications with the market on the part of SMEs and MNCs.
4 Give two examples of how cultural problems can affect international marketing negotiations and explain how these could be avoided.
5 Examine the relationships between some of the reasons given for the

failure of firms in international marketing. In your opinion, are these problems mainly of a tactical or of a strategic nature?

References

Connell, D. (ed.) (1979) The UK's performance in export marketing. NEDO paper.

McCall, J. and Warrington, B. (1984) *Marketing by Agreement*, John Wiley.

Tookey, D.E. (1964) Factors associated with success in exporting. *British Journal of Management*, March.

Turnbull, P.W. and Cunningham, M.T. (eds) (1981) *International Marketing and Purchasing*, Macmillan Press.

The impact of culture on international planning and implementation of marketing strategies

❏   CHAPTER PREVIEW

The chapter endeavours to emphasize the importance of culture to any international marketing operation. The various elements and social forces which cause a people to react in a certain way are analysed and, where possible, classified in their component parts.

Examples of these classifications and their effects upon marketing operations are shown and commented upon.

This chapter relates to various aspects of international marketing but in particular to promotion and sales.

❏   BY THE END OF THIS CHAPTER YOU SHOULD:

■   Be aware of the importance of culture in all aspects of inter-

■   national marketing

■   **Be able to analyse the various components and orientation of differing cultures**

■   **Avoid comparing your culture to other cultures**

■   **Perceive how aspects of other cultures affect the marketing mix and any marketing plans and operations.**   ❏

We start this chapter with a moving quotation from an African poet, which encapsulates the spirit of what culture is all about as well as affirming its importance as the essential characteristic of a people.

> Cultural activities are living in communion, by and within the community of other men. Culture is inside and outside, above and beneath all human activities: it is a spirit that animates them, that gives a civilization its unique style. We are now living in the final stage of world unification through interdependence.
>
> Senghor (Senegalese poet and former president of Senegal)

Whether in high diplomacy, business negotiations, personal relationships and human resource situations or down-to-earth market activities in foreign operations, the factor of the culture of the different parties is a crucial element. Wise diplomats and managers have long realized this and benefited where more obtuse operators have floundered owing to their inability to appreciate the importance of this factor. Hence any discussion on international matters, in this case the planning of international marketing operations, requires some detailed analysis and direction for the successful outcome of such ventures.

In this respect marketing borrows from anthropology and two definitions from notable anthropologists are a good basis for further analysis:

> The complex whole which includes knowledge, belief, art, morals, law, customs and any other capabilities and habits acquired by man as a member of society.
>
> E.B. Tylor (1891)

or

> The configuration of *learnt* behaviour and results of behaviour whose component elements are *shared* and *transmitted* by members of a particular society (author's italics)
>
> Ralph Linton (1945)

Another quotation, this time from a fellow marketer:

> The sum total of the ways of living built up by a group of human beings which is *transmitted* from one generation to another
>
>   i.e. Ideas
>
>   Attitudes
>
>   Values
>
>   Symbols
>
> (author's italics)
>
> Ralph Keegan in W.J. Keegan (1984)
> *Multinational Marketing Management*, 3rd edn, Prentice-Hall

The important factors, which are italicized in the above quotations, are that culture is peculiar to humankind inasmuch as it is both learnt and transmitted. The animal world performs even the most intricate activities and builds complex artefacts such as nests without learning how to do them; they are incorporated in their genes. Humans, however, learn their cultural norms from those around them. This is particularly important for the marketer as it implies that over time and in certain instances culture can be modified and overcome entrenched attitudes.

The problem created by the slow acceptance of tea bags and cold draught beer in the conservative UK society are two cases where a new product or idea has gained ground even against conservative opinion, eventually to gain acceptance. However, in more traditional cultures, such as in strict Moslem countries with their attitude to alcoholic drink and restraint towards the role of females in society, we find that cultural norms appear to remain firmly entrenched and are unlikely to change.

Broadly the dimensions of culture incorporated in Keegan's elements would comprise:

Religion   – the effect of this on attitudes and consumption
The family   – whether nuclear or extended and its role in a particular society
Education   – affecting consumers' use of a product as well as receiving communication about it
Social aspects – the social structure of a given society
Language   – the adhesive which binds the above together
Attitudes   – which are generated and established by the above

Briefly these are the basic definitions and dimensions of a culture. Using these as foundations for analysis, a structure of component factors, elements and orientations can be constructed in order to illustrate the importance and relevance of this subject for the marketer.

In effect, the culture of a people derives from their past experiences and efforts to respond to various problems arising from their environment. If proved successful these responses and concepts are passed on to future generations and become accepted as attitudes which govern their lives.

Figure 4.1 describes a comprehensive model which attempts to incorporate as many aspects of a people's background as possible with the assumption that these factors are like forces which result in a particular set of cultural norms and attitudes.

It cannot be stressed too highly that the disregard or neglect of any of those attitudes at best can embarrass a customer's feelings and still be passed off with a humorous exchange of apologies and compliments but at worst can be the reason for the total failure of a venture, with its resulting costs and losses.

Components of culture

The following aspects of culture as they affect all aspects of the marketing process – which incorporates marketing research, product design, promotion, distribution, planning and other functions – are each discussed in turn, with some examples of how they apply. The list is not exhaustive nor, apart from the most important area of language, set out in

Figure 4.1 Constituent elements of a culture

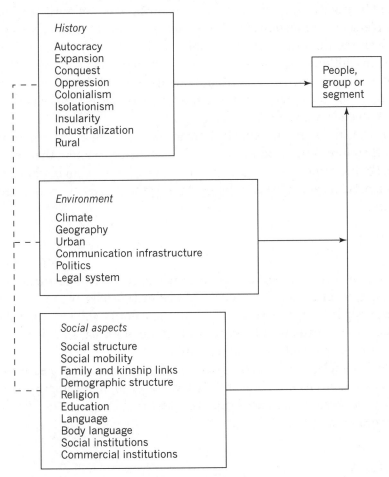

any order of importance. Furthermore, the level of impact varies with situations and the different components are also interrelated with one or more aspects, some of them affecting or being influenced by the others.

We start with one of the most prominent components.

Language

The problems connected with translation are legion, including the difficulties of avoiding brand names which can have offensive or negative meanings in another language. For example, GM's model, the Nova, could be translated as 'doesn't go' in Spanish. Also the word 'gift' which has pleasant connotations in English actually means 'poison' in German.

Even the English language common to Britain and the United States contains differences which can cause embarrassment or offence. The writer asked a class of American students not to borrow one another's rubbers, meaning pencil erasers, only to scandalize them since in the USA this term denotes a condom.

In fact, the Eastman Kodak company was well aware of this problem and therefore conducted extensive research before naming their product the Kodak camera so as not to have any adverse connotation in any foreign language, as well as being easily pronounced by people everywhere.

Body language

This term denotes the various ways in which certain cultures convey meaning by means of signs, shrugs, facial expressions or eye movement. Such body language varies from country to country and strangers should make it their business to be aware and attuned to what is really meant by any of these methods of communication.

For example, two fingers raised and parted can mean peace in one culture and an insulting defiance elsewhere. Also, in Northern Europe a nod of the head means an affirmative whereas in Bulgaria, for instance, it can mean a negative.

Religion

Religion is still a very powerful force in many societies and guides its adherents in all matters concerning rest days, fasting, diet, social customs, conduct of business and consumption patterns. Undertaking business trips or planning complex marketing campaigns during the month of Ramadan when people in Moslem countries fast from sunrise to sunset will certainly fail to gain enthusiastic response from local employees, agents or even customers.

In another instance, McDonalds were forced to change the nature of their main product, the beefburger, in India and replace it with chicken or vegetable-based products. As with language, above, this is a minefield of a subject and the market's religious intensity and make-up should be an early priority of study.

Social structure

This is the number, distribution and proportions of the social classes in a given society, together with the role and composition of the family, whether in its extended form or in the nuclear grouping more common to Western societies (i.e. father, mother and [sic] two point five children).

This also takes into account such factors as the degree and possibility of social mobility and mixing among classes: whether members of lower classes are able by means of education, connections or merit to join a higher social grouping or whether this cannot be achieved because of prevailing constraints upon individuals.

In the United States, for example, it is considered the norm for people to move to other parts of the country because of the requirements of their job. This may also entail promotion and advancement in social status. In other parts of the world, however, such as in India, people may still be bound in a rigid caste system which denies social advancement because of their background.

In such a culture, therefore, the marketers of certain products, such as books and other educational aids which seek to assist people to aspire to and achieve higher social as well as professional status, may find their attempts thwarted by the prevailing cultural climate of social hierarchy.

Similarly, in the domestic conditions of an extended family such activities as home study courses may prove impossible to follow.

Morals and ethics

This includes the roles and scope of females in a society, their degree of freedom of choice and expression and what would be considered proper or improper. The idea of unchaperoned females meeting male friends before marriage or the degree of toleration of females in various states of undress in advertisements is not acceptable in Moslem countries.

Also included are the close ties of the family as they are affected by and affect business, the degree of trust without written agreement or contract, and understanding of what is acceptable conduct, such as expectation of a reward for introduction or facilitation of an agreement. (Q. When is a bribe not a bribe?)

Products sold for the express purpose of gifts may not be practical when potential customers consider making presents to members of the opposite sex an immoral or impure act.

In the second instance, it may prove difficult and even impossible to gain access to an important business contact without distributing appropriate gifts to people who have close contact or influence with the desired person.

Demographics

This indicates the distribution of age, males and females or even social classes in the population. For instance, there is a much higher preponderance of minors in developing countries than in industrialized nations.

Perceived product benefits and usage

This is the demand for a product whether by size, quantity or volume, and also the use of a product; for example, the use of bicycles as either leisure or transportation goods depending upon the country where they are sold. Another instance is the use of pyjamas, sleepware in Europe but sold as walking-out lightweight leisure clothing in tropical countries like Egypt.

Political/legal system

Whether the government is a democracy, autocracy, oligarchy, theocracy, ruled by military junta or a ruling group or family, and the outcome of the legal system imposed by any of these and its effect upon the marketing process. (For example, Shariah Law in Moslem countries and its strict prohibition of the sale of alcohol. Also, the hours during which shops, banks or businesses are allowed to open, etc.)

Attitudes

These are existing attitudes to products, whether they are xenophobic towards imported foreign goods or the degree of popularity of certain styles and colours, designs, etc.

The attitudes also relate to many other factors in a culture and will be discussed further in a separate analysis.

History

This is the historic background of a country or region which may comprise wars, occupation, colonialism, oppression or alliances and its resultant effect on attitudes and national characteristics. For example, Portugal regards itself as England's oldest ally and has always been disposed towards trade with the UK because of its fear, until recent times, of its large neighbour, Spain.

Symbols

This is the veneration and respect for, or hostility to, certain symbols and designs, for example stars, crosses, animals, figures, designs (e.g. a mythical animal such as a dragon or a design such as a crescent); also, any other items which may have an emotional impact or generate sentimental feelings among the population have to be seriously considered in any form of communication.

The Greek people were very angry and made strong representations to Coca-Cola about what an outsider might consider quite a harmless and witty advertisement. The design of the advertisement was a drawing which showed the Parthenon in Athens supported by four typical Coke bottles instead of Greek Corinthian columns. This trivial approach to a cherished national monument made the Greeks very indignant and eventually forced Coca-Cola to withdraw the advertisement, although not before losing many sales and much goodwill in Greece.

Similarly, the Christian Dior fashion house caused much consternation in the Arab world because of a dress design that had verses from the Koran as a decoration.

Such lapses in judgement, or insensitivity towards cultural feelings, can cost companies dearly.

Clothing

Although most nationalities nowadays wear Western dress, there are certain occasions and places where the mode of dress indicates status in the community, professional standing, social obligation or a distinct cultural identity. The wearing of robes, uniforms, kilts, turbans, kimonos, stetsons, dinner jacket and black tie are all examples of dress for both cultural and specific occasions. In all cases the wearer makes a statement about his or her status, profession, occasion, social milieu or position in society.

Experience

This is similar to historic background but more primaeval in its effects or outcomes. It may give rise to such attitudes as collective security and desire for male offspring, reticence and distrust of strangers or authority as a result of the effect of previous societal experience upon the collective mind. Such attitudes may affect certain pharmaceutical products or services such as insurance or banking.

Education

This is the degree of literacy in a given population which enables the use of newspaper advertisements and other promotional programmes as well as the use of subtle messages in an advertisement's copy or artwork, such as the Benson & Hedges and Silk Cut advertisements.

It is also the ability to conceptualize abstract ideas or obtain satisfaction from certain products, such as the ability to operate and obtain benefit from the use of computers, or other sophisticated capital goods.

Aesthetics

This is the acceptance of the norm of what is considered beauty in a certain culture. For example, African art or surrealism which appeals to subcultures and is likely to affect such items as packaging, product design and advertising.

Customs and etiquette

This is the folk ways or mores of a people, such as handshakes, dressing for dinner, kissing a lady's hand or kissing on both cheeks; the giving of gifts or the sending of greetings cards on occasions. The mutual presentation of visiting cards by business partners and the polite preliminaries prior to any round of negotiations are some examples of local customs.

Rituals and ceremonies

These are occasions which call for a certain memorable record in some formal social procedure. Examples are weddings, retirements, product launches, agency appointments, promotions or other events which call for some form of celebration or formalized process which can be remembered and referred to in the future.

Manners

This is the accepted form of correct procedure in social gatherings. When meeting, greeting, eating or attending some other social occasion, such procedures as bowing, standing, use of utensils, etc. can vary and cause offence if the visitor does not come prepared. For instance, it is quite proper and expected in some societies for a guest to belch, or emit wind, after a meal to show appreciation to the host or hostess – a procedure which would result in total ostracism in Western society.

Superstitions

Although illogical and irrational, such matters as being thirteenth at table or seeing a black cat cross one's path can cause discomfort for some people. Promotions and occasions at which such conditions occur should be avoided even though they may appear ridiculous or unimportant to a stranger in a host country.

The casting of horoscopes at the outset of a business venture is taken very seriously by many people and should not be underestimated by business partners.

Entertainments and leisure pursuits

This includes the preference of different societies for certain preferred sports or entertainments, e.g. bullfighting in Spain and Mexico, opera in Italy, ballet in Russia or English pantomime with its peculiar traditions. Skiing, football and golf are universally acclaimed sports but enjoy more popularity in some countries than others. They are also enjoyed by different social groups within a society and serve to segment the target market. They all provide a useful base for identifying ideal promotional and public relations activities.

This list is not exhaustive and, as mentioned above, can be both inter-related and even separated into further component parts. Examples abound as regards the failures and losses where such factors were ignored or not given sufficient consideration.

For instance, the British subsidiary of a multinational pharmaceutical corporation developed a cure for certain skin ailments. This was a powder, or a lotion to be mixed with the bath water when sufferers took a bath. It was successful in the United Kingdom but failed abysmally in France, where the preference is to shower rather than take baths.

Similarly, the French subsidiary of this same corporation developed a suppository pill for certain ailments which was successful in France where such a form of cure is commonplace. In the United Kingdom, patients who were prescribed such a cure thought they were pills and complained to their doctor that they were too big to swallow. They were very shocked when they were informed of the correct manner of application of a suppository, such methods of cure being considered shocking and totally opposed to British culture and usage. (See Figure 4.2.)

The varied and various components of culture as listed and discussed above result in a people adopting certain attitudes. These in turn affect such patterns as purchasing, domestic planning, employment and various other matters which all impinge upon the marketing process.

When discussing culture, however, it should be noted that this is a developing process and cultures do evolve over time. Also, any given society has a number of subcultures each with their own attitudes and norms. For instance, the youth culture of the Western world adopts many forms of aesthetics, product usage and attitudes quite separate from those of their parents' culture. Furthermore, elements of this subculture are spread worldwide and are adopted by young people of a certain age, albeit with adaptation and superimposition of their own ethnic culture. Doubtless this will, in time, become a development of the national culture but it is observed that when young people mature they usually revert to adopting the customs of their country.

Figure 4.2 You what?

The adoption or assumption of a culture by an individual, group or nation will result in a set of accepted attitudes. When analysing culture, therefore, as well as classifying its various components as above, a classification of its concomitant attitudes gives further insight into the way a people would react to certain products or concepts introduced by a marketer from another country and culture.

The following, somewhat stark and simplistic list endeavours to classify some of these attitudes in order to act as a guide and way of understanding a foreign culture.

Cultural attitudes

These attitudes, which may result from any of the above-mentioned components of a culture, can be summarized as follows:

● **Attitude towards work and achievement** The Protestant Ethic, i.e. the feeling that one must live to work and that work brings an intrinsic reward. The 'work ethic' and the status achieved by working.

- **Attitude towards the role of the sexes and sexual discrimination**   Where a culture holds that a woman's place is in the home and has specifically allocated roles and occupations as well as prohibiting, or frowning upon, the association of mixed groups; such exclusion also extending to the exposure of the female form, either as worn in clothing or as presented in pictures.

- **Attitude towards the future**   The feeling that one may shape the future by planning for a desirable outcome as against the opposite view of an unalterable future already decided and decreed by fate and divine forces. The 'Kismet' mentality of acceptance of events.

- **Attitude towards authority**   The acceptance of an all-wise and all-powerful authority by subordinates. As manifested in:

  (a)   The subordinate's expectation of direct command and no expectation of delegation in decision-making situations. This can be the cause of confusion between a foreign manager from a more liberal or entrepreneurial culture, accustomed to giving his or her subordinates as much scope as possible, and employees from more autocratic societies puzzling as to why their manager will not give straight directives.

  (b)   Reaction to policy directives. Similar to the above but applicable to managers of traditional cultures who see any suggestion or qualification to a directive from subordinates as a slur or insubordination. Any reaction other than immediate deference is seen by the manager as an implication of his or her inefficiency.

  (c)   Patterns of hierarchy in certain societies, e.g.:

    (i)   The class structure   The distribution of aristocratic or ruling class, upper, middle, artisan, peasant or nomadic groups within a society.

    (ii)   The context of caste   Conditions, either social or legal, which set a rigid pattern on class, occupation or residence on certain members of the population.

    (iii)   The 'glass ceiling'   Conditions imposed to prevent certain members of a society (e.g. female employees in certain occupations or people from working-class origins) rising in the social or professional hierarchy.

This attitude also manifests itself in the suspicion of all those in authority, and extends beyond the workplace to the government and to all strangers, who could be informers. Information is thus not imparted willingly except to those within the close family circle or peer group.

- **Family or tribal responsibility**
  - (a) The conflict in some societies between corporate aims to obtain the most suitable employee or contract and the expectation by the family that a manager should give preference to a relative or member of a particular community with whom he is associated.
  - (b) This conflict is manifested in situations when the profit motive is deemed secondary to the family or tribal loyalty.

- **Attitude towards time**   Societies where the concept of 'time is money' is the norm as against cultures which are more laid back and do not see the need for strict time keeping or time management.

  Similarly the attitude of 'business before pleasure', where functional duties are paramount and leisure pursuits only take place after those duties are completed. This attitude is also in evidence before negotiations begin, some cultures deliberately setting a period for amicable and personal conversation on non-business topics to set the tone of the meeting. Any attempt to hasten the proceedings will be viewed with great disapproval.

- **Attitude towards education**   The desirability or rejection of the acquisition of knowledge and the perception of its outcomes or benefits. Among certain groups the pursuit of knowledge may be considered as a waste of time which can be put to better use in the production of tangible artefacts.

- **Attitude towards industry and industrial undertakings and occupations**   Where industry and employment in industry are seen by some people as demeaning and unfit for persons of good family, refinement and education. This can be illustrated by the contempt felt by the upper class in Victorian times for those people who were 'in trade'. Some persistence of this attitude still remains as seen in the relatively low demand for engineering courses in Great Britain, the birthplace of the Industrial Revolution.

- **Attitude towards foreign goods** (xenophobia)   Some cultures seem to prefer foreign-manufactured products to those produced at home while in other countries there is staunch loyalty to domestic goods.

- **Attitude towards the taking of risk**   The urge to invest in business ventures rather than to accept the status quo. This is somewhat related and in contrast to the fatalistic acceptance of conditions as mentioned above in the attitude towards the future.
- **Attitude towards deferred satisfaction**   The putting to one side of immediate gratification, in the form of spending disposable income or leisure time, so as to obtain greater benefits at some later date.

   This attitude of deferred satisfaction with the habit of saving and frugality as against immediate gratification, extravagance and squandering of one's income could be linked with the attitude towards risk, mentioned above, as well as the attitude towards work or the 'Protestant Ethic' which is very strong in some societies. Such an attitude may be as a result of history or experience, as mentioned in the above components of culture.

The approval of or indifference to any of these attitudes in a society is an attitude in itself and forms part of the cultural norm.

Cultural orientations

As well as generating the attitudes discussed above, culture, because of its component factors, will also affect its members and adherents with a particular outlook or orientation.

Thus another cultural analysis, which may yet cover the same ground but still offer the marketer another insight into a potential investment, is by considering **cultural orientation** as an identification of consumers' and/or business partners' tendencies and predilections.

Aesthetic orientation

This is love of the arts, type of music and folklore of a particular people, and the nature and extent of symbolism in the art and traditions of a people.

For example, Esso's successful worldwide 'Tiger in the Tank' campaign had to be modified in certain Asian countries which saw the tiger as a sacred mythical animal as distinct from the cartoon character portrayed in the advertisements.

In another context of cultural orientation, the use of operatic arias as a background for British Airways' television commercials is appropriate to the culture of the target market which uses that product or service.

Time orientation

This is the importance given to the use of time by a societal group. In Western culture the concept of 'time is money' is regarded with an almost religious fervour whereas in the non-industrialized world the need to get 'down to business' hurriedly is seen as a breach of good manners.

Space orientation

The need for privacy, distance and mobility either in one's personal life or in collective social situations differs in importance with culture.

Such a classification can be taken a number of ways. Some cultures tend to be open in their overt discussion of personal or business matters while others tend to keep as much information as possible confidential. Also, the physical distance between persons varies with cultural usage. Northern Europeans tend to want to speak to other people with a space between them while in the Middle East nearness to one's addressee shows desire for friendship and sociability.

Mobility orientation

This can be regarded either as social mobility within a society or as the preference to gather in groups. The comfort of group cohesion is evident in some cultures or subcultures, such as the family, street corner gangs or locals in a pub.

There are alternative cultures, such as that of the United States, which is a society of socially mobile individuals in pursuit of totally opposite aims. This is referred to in the following subsection on societal orientation.

Societal orientation

Western societies tend to cultivate an attitude of individualistic orientation. Individuals are encouraged by their peers and the media to strike out for themselves and forge ahead. Such attitudes are not universal; the collectivism of more traditional societies fosters a deference and obligation to the general consensus, whether immediate family or the wider society.

The successful growth of Japanese business has been the result of the combination of traditional collective values merged with entrepreneurial acumen.

Material orientation

This is the degree of importance that members of a society put upon the ownership of material possessions. The ownership of cars, houses, articles of clothing, etc. is of great importance among members of certain social groups, while other groups may put relatively little value upon the possession of material goods apart from the day-to-day usage of certain products.

For those materialistic groups or sub-segments of a market the ownership of a good is a satisfaction in itself. The use of material goods can be of secondary importance. People could purchase an expensive car and rarely drive it, or a computer with many facilities which are not particularly necessary, but both those cases indicate the satisfaction gained from pure ownership rather than functional performance of the product.

Such orientation may only affect small groups within a culture. Paradoxically, a society may be mainly unimpressed by materialism due to unsophistication and technical retardment yet include within itself a small elite group who will assert themselves by, among other expressions of exclusivity, manifestations of a materialistic nature and a flaunting of luxurious possessions.

Spiritual/ideological orientation

This factor is directly opposed to the above and emphasizes the importance some cultures place upon mystical and abstract thought, religious or metaphysical contemplation, even superstitious beliefs, all serving to minimize the emphasis on acquisition of possessions.

Such orientation could also apply in groups who are highly politically as well as religiously motivated, where the pursuit of goals of power and proselytization are paramount.

Technical orientation

Cultures can be greatly affected by technology. Where people are accustomed to the use of certain sophisticated manufactured goods, the demand for certain attributes of a product will vary according to the priorities brought about by their use. For instance, the demand for more powerful computers is caused by the need for more economical use of time.

Similarly, energy saving preoccupies the Western world as a result of greater use of power-driven machines. This is in contrast to some other cultures where manpower is cheap and abundant, resulting in greater labour-intensive product demand.

The importance, therefore, of such concepts as maintenance procedures, reuse, repair and recycling of products and the opposing views of the 'throw-away society' are all manifestations of technology superimposed upon a culture.

Cultural identity

The self-appraisal of a society and the ways that its people see themselves, their social behaviour, work patterns and attitudes towards choice of products, in fact all those elements which a marketer identifies as determination of a target group, are all factors which confirm a specific culturally identifiable group.

A culture is generated by historical antecedents. A long history and heritage will evoke traditions and traditional ways of thinking. More recent social groupings, such as those brought together by immigration or political resolution, evolve their own traditions and norms. In time they will also find their own peculiar traditions.

Possibly culture could be viewed as a reaction by a certain group of people to environmental conditions. The need for male offspring, for instance, could be attributed to the time when old age pensions did not exist and one looked to one's children for support in old age. Countries in the Third World wishing to pursue family planning programmes are particularly hampered by the resistance of their populations because of a culture which relates to past conditions and is not convinced by current assurances.

Marketers will have to develop extreme sensitivity to the feelings and outlooks of such culturally identifiable entities which, despite their extensive historical past in some cases, are still in a constant state of evolution and progression. As mentioned above, some facets of those cultures can be adapted to suit the consumption of certain goods and services, while others remain, for the foreseeable future, quite immutable and resistant to change.

Cereal breakfast foods, which originated in the United States, have become largely accepted in place of traditional cooked breakfasts in the United Kingdom, mainly for convenience in today's busy lifestyle, but so far the acceptance of iced tea, another American product, by the British public has been very slow.

Thus cultural identity incorporates most of the components, attitudes and orientations which we have discussed. Language, mode of dress, social structure and many other factors go towards emphasizing a nation's particular and peculiar identity. National pride as well as an inherent trait of human nature gives people a tendency towards a cultural identity.

It should be noted that cultural identity need not affect the total population of one country. Within a broad national culture, various reference groups, subcultures or sub-segments of the market may exist, each of which have their specific traits. For example, teenagers, personnel in the armed forces, mining communities, seamen, farm workers or university students, each of whom comprise a subsection of the population and have their own peculiarities of dress, taste, idiomatic speech and attitudes.

Sometimes such cultural groups tend to spread horizontally across national boundaries, such as the so-called jet-set or certain professions and trades who adopt recognizable norms as suggested above wherever they happen to live.

Summing up

From the above, far from exhaustive applications of culture one can discern a broad analytic logic. Since, as mentioned above, culture could be seen as a people's response to certain environmental conditions and possibly was a means of survival in the past, it is not an issue which can be either dismissed lightly or taken as an eccentric foible. There is, however, no easy answer or identifiable reason for every circumstance and many cultural variables are the result of conditions either deeply buried in the past or purely symbolic in their manifestation. Nevertheless, culture forms a basic plank in the understanding of the foreign consumer and the marketer must build upon this slender platform to appreciate his or her customer's or trading partner's reactions to what are, to the marketer, alien conditions.

Ethnocentrism, which is the attitude that what is suitable for the home market is vastly superior, eminently desirable and consequently to be offered as ideally suitable for the target market, is to be avoided. Such an attitude is totally contrary to the marketing concept and equally ignores the principle of consumer satisfaction. For example, the British motorcycle industry lost ground to the Japanese for not considering foreign (and later on even British) preferences for motorcycles with electric starters and other refinements offered by the Japanese competition.

Advertisements and promotions that are accepted and successful in one's home culture may, at best, be ignored and the message misunderstood but at worst give real offence, which may lose the company business.

As an example of this misunderstanding which went sour, a British tyre manufacturer, wanting to make a statement about the durability of their product and its beneficial effect on petrol consumption, ran a supposedly humorous advertisement depicting an enraged Arab sheikh being deprived of his petroleum royalties.

The result of the publication of such an innocuous (to the British public) picture was outrage by many Arab countries, who promptly cancelled orders for this and other products. Thus what seemed a harmless joke led to orders worth thousands of pounds being lost.

The manifestation of the above attitude, therefore, is the practice, to be avoided at all costs in international marketing, of the **self-reference criterion** or SRC. This is the feeling that other people's reactions are the same as one's own on the sole basis of one's own ways of thinking and appreciation. Awareness of many of the above-mentioned orientations and attitudes must form the basis of any marketing plan in an international context.

Essentially the marketer must consider culture and give it due importance among the many other variables that affect any marketing operation. In domestic marketing operations, cultural norms are taken for granted and such aspects of marketing as consumer behaviour are adapted to the situation as it occurs with the consumers in the market. Thus in international marketing an extra dimension allowing for culture has to be superimposed upon the marketing mix.

For example, taking only some cultural factors, the four Ps of the marketing mix can be affected by a society's culture in the following ways:

- Product
  - (a) Product design – whether capital or labour intensive
    - acceptable colour scheme
    - aesthetically pleasing to the culture
    - size of pack
  - (b) Product usage – whether seen as luxury or commonplace good
    - whether seen as restricted for certain groups (e.g. wine for adults only)
    - whether seen as a leisure or occupational product (e.g. bicycles, heavy-duty boots, etc.)
- Price – prevalence of bargaining
    - attitude towards imported products
    - expectation of extra benefits (e.g. discounts, guarantee, service, delivery, etc.)
- Place – preference of venues (e.g. bazaars, shopping malls, etc.)
    - facilities for women shoppers (e.g. changing rooms)
    - acceptance of certain consumers (e.g. children in bars)
- Promotion – display of female body
    - linguistic confusion in translation
    - ethnic origin of actors in TV commercials
    - scepticism or acceptance of the advertiser's message

The above are just brief examples of how culture affects the various marketing functions (see Figure 4.3). Various examples and discussions elsewhere will elaborate this very important factor.

In conclusion, the analysis and understanding of culture is a vast subject covered by many books on anthropology and sociology as well as international business and marketing. This chapter attempts to show its crucial importance to the business and marketing process. Not every cultural attitude or individual culture can be identified here but a broad analysis is provided and an outline of various examples of cultural

Figure 4.3 Impact of culture on marketing decisions. (Adapted from Jain's model in *International Marketing Management*, Kent Publishing Co, Boston, 1984.)

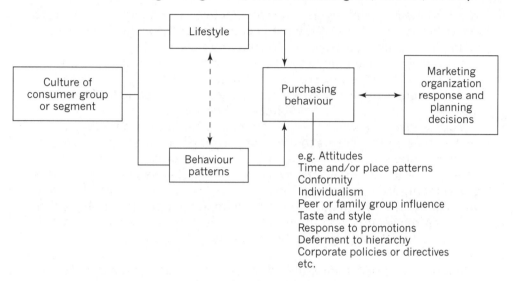

disparities is displayed, which hopefully will guide the student to the awareness of the pitfalls which lie in wait for the unwary marketer.

Chapter review

Culture is a most important attribute of a people. Many instances show that a people's culture will affect their attitudes and actions. This is especially relevant to commercial transactions, buying and selling and therefore marketing. The international marketer has to be very sensitive to this factor in all operations.

Culture is a learnt attribute, unlike the animal kingdom where actions and modes of existence are inherent in the genes. Human beings learn their culture and ways of life. Such aspects as language, attitudes, religious observances and moral codes are learnt by members of a society from those around rather than bred into them.

Culture could be said to arise from past experience, geography and the environment. A number of factors or components are listed and commented upon. This is not an exhaustive list, nor are the items separate but are, in most cases, interlinked. Furthermore, these components give

Mini Case study

The McDonald's hamburgers international television campaign has come under fire in Israel, one of the many countries which show a televised commercial produced originally for the American market. The commercial television film shows a hamburger being assembled with slices of cheese added to produce the final product. This has evoked protests from orthodox groups in Israel because the eating of cheese and meat at the same time is prohibited by their religion.

McDonalds, who stress that all the meat used in their hamburgers is kosher, that is, it conforms to the religious preparation and processing of meat, maintain that it is a small minority who protest and that it has political, rather than religious overtones. The religious parties in Israel's government, according to McDonalds, want to flex their political muscle and show that they can impose their will upon the way the country is run.

Editing the sequence of the film by cutting out the insertion of the cheese into the hamburger has been suggested but ruled out as being too expensive.

McDonalds have run into difficulties with religious groups over their products before now, with regular picketing of their restaurants by orthodox Jews. In fact, viewpoints are divided on this matter, with some people seeing the entry of McDonalds as a symbol of consumer prosperity and others as the loss of the country's cultural soul.

(This case has been adapted from an article in *The Daily Telegraph*, 8 October 1996).

Questions

1   What aspects of culture and marketing are involved in this case?
2   What do you think are the underlying reasons for this problem?
3   Is there anything that McDonalds could do about the situation?

rise to attitudes and feelings which affect the choice, desire and selection of products and therefore have to be given serious consideration in all marketing plans.

Questions

Section A: Class discussion

1   'The world is becoming smaller and therefore cultural factors should not matter in international marketing operations.' Discuss.
2   In any given marketing situation, using actual or fictitious illustrations, comment upon the outcome of the concept of time and space orientation.
3   What external factors go towards the assimilation of a culture and its particular attitudes?
4   Some neighbouring countries display important cultural differences despite their proximity. Why do you think this is so?
5   To what extent are cultural barriers greater than linguistic barriers? Use examples to illustrate your answer.

Section B: Examination revision

1   'Functional products do not encounter cultural differences as a rule.' Discuss, using examples to support your arguments.
2   What lessons can anthropologists give to international marketers and how do you think these may be applied?
3   Compare religious with educational differences and their effect on purchasing patterns.
4   'The extended family is both advantageous and a hindrance to marketing operations.' Discuss.
5   Why are SRC and ethnocentricity particularly damaging to any foreign operation? Illustrate your answer with examples of these.

References

Jain, S.C. (1984) *International Marketing Management*, Boston: Kent Publishing Co.

McCall, I. and Warrington, B. (1984) *Marketing by Agreement*, John Wiley.

Usunier, J.-P. (1996) *Marketing Across Cultures*, Prentice-Hall.

5

Market selection strategy, international market research and the European Union

❏ CHAPTER PREVIEW

The three topics of this chapter are highly interactive and interdependent. While the market selection strategy will often depend largely on the fit between organization/product and the characteristics of the market, international marketing research is essential to determine the situation in that market. Specific barriers and opportunities play a major role, and the influence of a free trade association may be important in this context.

These topics are related particularly to long-term planning, market entry strategy and the technical aspects of international marketing.

❏ BY THE END OF THIS CHAPTER YOU SHOULD:

■ Understand the different kinds of constraints on market selection strategy

■ Understand the significance of trade barriers and opportunities

■ **Understand the significance of fit between the organization/ product and the potential market**

■ **Understand that one company may have very different strategies for different markets**

■ **Be aware of the costs and benefits of international marketing research**

■ **Be aware of the growing and differing roles of Free Trade Associations throughout the world**

■ **Be aware of the economic and political developments of the European Union.** ❏

Market selection strategies

The basis of these is formed in the long-term planning of the organization for overseas markets. Without investment in terms of finance and human resources, the firm is unlikely to succeed internationally. After the budget has been decided, the next step is to prioritize the markets.

Fit between organization and the specific market

The most important single factor in market selection strategy is to ensure the fit between the organization, its management style, its product and the specific market. It is therefore dangerous to generalize about markets without considering specific products and companies as well as the specific market. This is because a market which may be ideal for one product may be totally unsuitable for another due to market entry barriers or some other problem. (See Figure 5.1.)

Research shows that medium-sized firms have greater success rates when they target a smaller number of markets which are new for them rather than 'have a go' at a large number. This is known as Key Market Entry Strategy. Initially, secondary desk research is needed on potential

Figure 5.1 Comparative factors for market selection. (Adapted from Majaro's *International Market Profile Analysis*.)

Market profile analysis

	Product	Price	Distribution	Promotion	Personal sales
Country A Product X					
Environment Consumer behaviour Cultural aspects Geography Climate Industrial and Economic Development etc.					
Competition					
Legal system					
Institutions					
Other factors					

Country B Product X

Environment
Consumer behaviour
Cultural aspects
Geography
Climate
Industrial and
Economic
Development etc.
Competition
Legal system
Institutions
Other factors

Country C Product X

Environment
Consumer behaviour
Cultural aspects
Geography
Climate
Industrial and
Economic
Development
Competition
Legal system
Institutions
Other factors

Country D Product X

Environment
Consumer behaviour
Cultural aspects
Geography
Climate
Industrial and
Economic
Development
Competition
Legal system
Institutions
Other factors

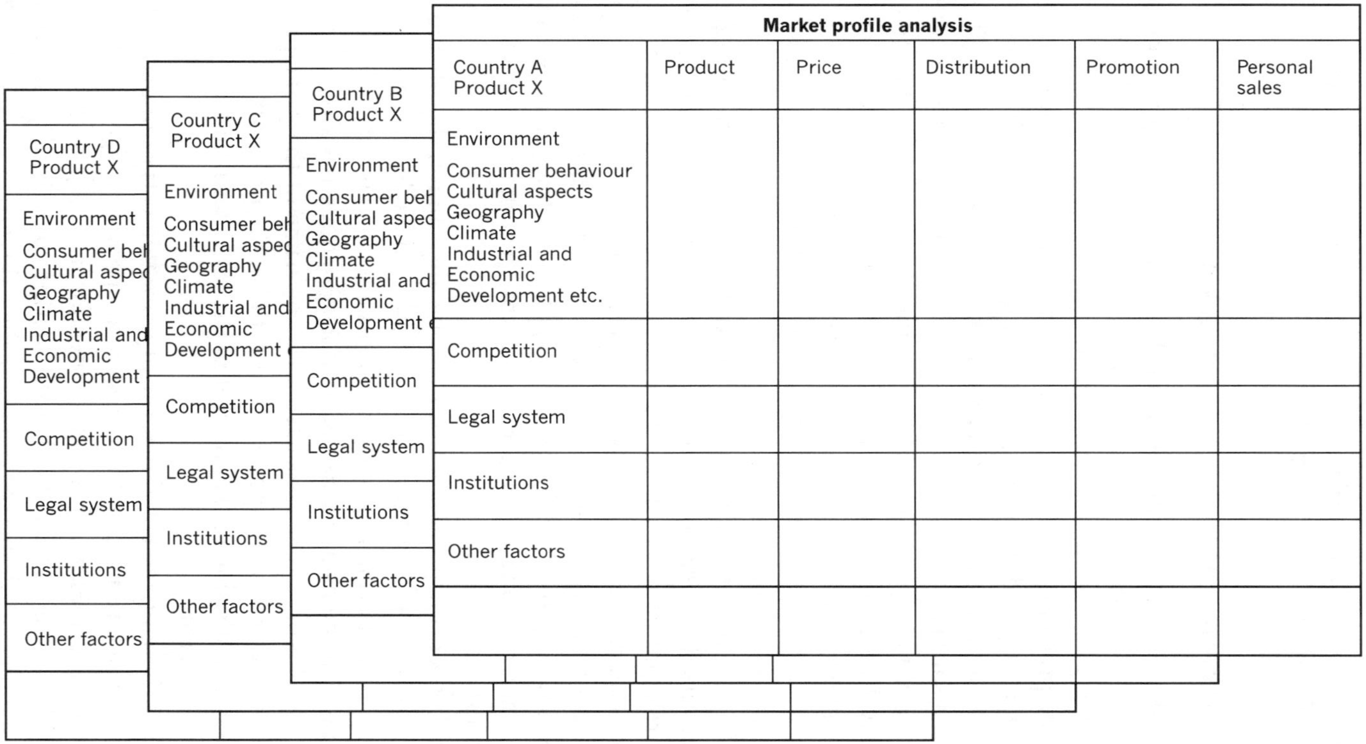

markets before any serious and more expensive primary research is carried out on the target market.

The significance of timely market research

Why do successful firms not select their agent or distributor first and let them do the market research? The intermediary is arguably in a better position to carry out research on the market.

The problem with this approach is that the long-term interests of the intermediary and the principal may be quite different. The intermediary may prefer a medium turnover with a price skimming policy. This would need a smaller salesforce usually. However, the long-term interest of the principal may be for a much larger turnover and a market penetration policy. But the most crucial problem of selecting the intermediary is that the appointment of an agent or distributor is arguably the most important decision with regard to the success of the market entry strategy in that particular market.

We will now examine the problems that arise when an organization discovers that it has appointed the wrong agent. In most cases the law of the relevant country will afford the agent substantial protection against dismissal, so that, regardless of the terms of the contract, the principal will have to pay considerable damages to the agent. In addition, the principal may suffer serious loss of reputation. Other good agents may be reluctant to come forward to represent the company in that market. Patriotic feelings can run high.

When a principal appoints the 'wrong' distributor, the situation can be even worse. A distributor usually has a much higher profile than an agent, often having large display rooms and an extensive salesforce. This means that the name of the distributor, who often has a very high profile, can also become very associated with the name of the principal. Therefore, in the case of a rupture between them, the principal is likely to face a loss of reputation in that market in the short term and a loss of sales in the long term.

It is therefore essential that the organization carry out detailed market research before it takes the decision to appoint an agent. This research may indeed indicate that some other form of approach to that market would be better. It may be that the market could be approached directly by sending a salesperson there to deal directly with buyers. Another solution might be a takeover of a local firm, with the idea of using their marketing expertise and knowledge of the market. Market entry strategy will be discussed in depth in Chapters 6 and 7, but market research is an essential preliminary step, and this will be examined in the next section but one.

Market entry barriers

Some of the factors that can lead to the elimination of a particular market from one's considerations are market entry barriers. These barriers include tariffs, quotas and cultural barriers.

Certain countries forbid the importation of certain goods. Whisky or any other form of alcoholic beverage may not be imported into Saudi Arabia. Other countries have widely differing laws concerning the importation of foods. Other problems can arise in the packaging of one's products and this problem will be examined in greater depth in Chapter 12 on technical aspects. While packaging can be a problem for many international marketers, it is above all a problem for manufacturers of packaging materials, particularly as the legislation in this respect is constantly changing. More and more countries are banning the use of plastics of all types in packaging because of the increasing threat to our environment by CFCs, both in their manufacture and also in the safe disposal of them.

It is essential to detect important market entry barriers early on, before valuable time is wasted on too much market research which internationally can be very expensive.

Market research

We stated earlier that effective market research is essential in international marketing. We will now examine some of the most important aspects of that market research, starting with some definitions:

The systematic gathering, recording, analysis and interpretation of data on problems relating to the market for, and the marketing of, goods and services

The process of analysis and idea generation which leads to ascertaining what information will be most useful for the marketing of a product; the most cost-effective way of obtaining the most relevant information to meet these ends

The all-important thing is to make sure in advance that you know exactly what it is you are gathering data for:

- Is it to solve a problem?
- Is it to give you a picture of the competition in the market?
- Is it to inform you about the role of agents/distributors in that particular market?

More money and energy are wasted in market research because principals do not know exactly what they want to know or because they do not formulate their needs accurately enough. These questions need to be formulated accurately, irrespective of whether the firm is carrying out the research itself, or employing another firm to do it.

Secondary research

This is the search for information from relevant data already available. This data could take the form of information from censuses or information readily available from telephone or industry directories.

Primary research

This is the obtaining of information specifically for current and future needs.

In most market research projects the following stages can be recognized:

1   Definition of opportunity or problem
2   Decision on usefulness of market research
3   Definition of preliminary scope of research

The following process usually takes place:

1   Preparation of terms of reference
2   Research design
3   Information collection
4   Analysis and interpretation of data
5   Research report and conclusions

6 Marketing decision
7 Implementation

Some differences between secondary market research in international marketing compared with the domestic scene

Expertise

First of all, specific expertise is required over and above that needed in the domestic market. This expertise will include specific knowledge of the market, including any relevant languages and culture.

Extra cost

Thorough market research cannot be hurried so extra cost may be involved, especially if the cost of living in the specific market is above average, as a stay of some months in the country may be necessary to gather all the relevant information.

Unreliability of information

In many countries of the world, reliable information may be difficult to obtain due to several factors:

- Rarity of censuses
- Non-existence of censuses
- Material out of date
- Government interference with data
- Data in a foreign language or not in correct format
- Strong regional differences within the country

In addition, culturally sophisticated interpretation of the data may be required. If, for example, the sales of certain goods in one region is suspiciously high, does this mean that some of the goods are being consumed in another region, or even exported out of the country?

Forecasting

The process of predicting the future is like a person driving a car, blindfold, following instructions from someone looking out the rear window. Much of forecasting is based on history. Yet history rarely repeats itself in the same pattern. In addition, the business world is changing so rapidly that very few firms rely on the past to predict the future. However, companies need to attempt to forecast and that is where an intimate knowledge of the market can help in estimating future trends there.

In the last chapter we saw some of the problems which arise in overseas market research due to cultural differences.

But, while many of the major problems of marketing research in international marketing are due to external factors, many mistakes are due to classical management errors such as insufficient analysis of what information is needed, how much is needed and how exactly it will be used.

Use of the 'salami method' (Figure 5.2) is essential due to generally higher costs. This means carrying out research in slices, so that you do not commit too much money to research on one particular market at one time, which may be totally unsuitable.

Free trade associations

Free trade associations are nothing new. Ancient Greece had something very similar and the German Hanseatic League of states had a similar idea. This idea is that unity is strength and that if, by forming a union, you can export your goods more easily then it will benefit your state and its citizens. After the Second World War, some eminent European statesmen, including Schumann, had the idea that if the nations of Western Europe could form a 'Bund', firstly it would put a stop to the incessant wars, and secondly it would foster trade and prosperity. Today there are many free trade associations in the world:

- North American Free Trade Agreement
- MERCOSUR
- Association of South East Asian Nations
- CARICOM (CARIBBEAN COMMON MARKET)
- Arab/Middle East Arab Common Market

Figure 5.2 The 'Salami' method of evaluating stages of the research process, with due regard to resource and expenditure considerations

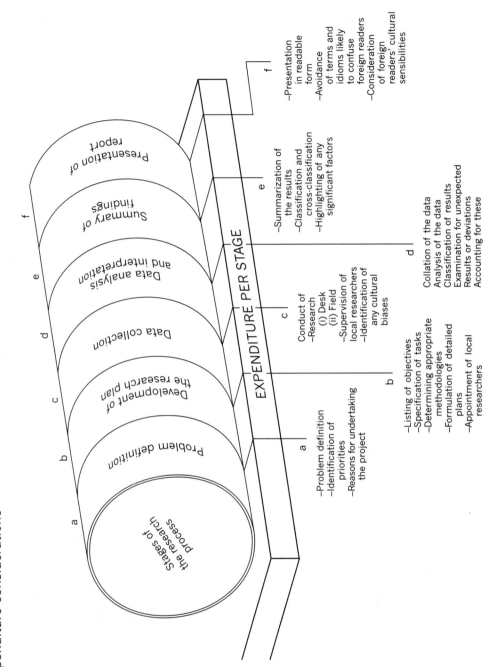

The above are but a few of the many, and the tendency today is for such associations to grow in number and in strength. Using a reference book, find out which countries belong to any five free trade associations.

The European Union

The formation and development of the European Union has not only greatly changed the lives of all the citizens within it, but is very fast becoming a model for other groups of nations to try to emulate (Figure 5.3).

The formation and development of this union has been much quicker than many politicians would have foreseen after the Second World War. In 1945 intelligent politicians asked themselves how to prevent another war. These had been occurring with monotonous regularity, and Germany and France were involved in all of them. From the battle of Waterloo in 1815, only 55 years elapsed until the Franco-Prussian War. The Great War, as it was called, started in 1914, followed by the

Figure 5.3 Aims of the European Union and the Single European Act

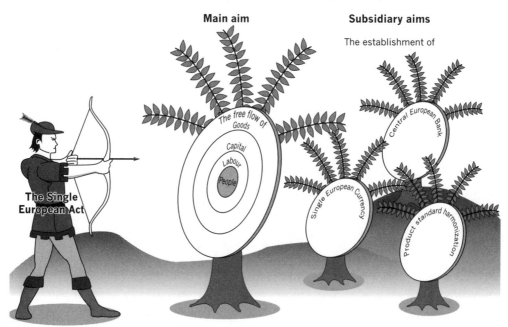

Second World War in 1939–45. Some of the leading politicians such as Schumann believed the key to future peace in Europe lay in cooperation and alliances which would make war, especially between the chief protagonists, impossible. Up until then the coal and steel industries had been the driving force of war. The American civil war was won in the factories of the North as much as the battlefields. So a major idea was the formation of the Coal and Steel Community, which would bring the main adversaries, France and Germany, together.

Here is a list of some of the developments of the EU. If you want to know more details, there is a resource list at the end of the chapter. It is important to understand the EU in its historical context. It was originally conceived as a political, not just an economic idea. The fact that it was originally called the European Economic Community confused some people into believing that it was intended to be merely a free trade association. But the founders of the European Union always intended that it should become much more.

1947 Post-war US Marshall Plan aid programme prompts the establishment of the Organization of European Economic Cooperation (OEEC).

1948 Netherlands, Belgium and Luxembourg join in the Benelux Union, a construction considered by many as the blue-print for EU development.
Treaty of Brussels initiates the Western European Union (WEU), a 50-year-old agreement between Belgium, the Netherlands, France, Luxembourg and the UK.

1949 Council of Europe created in Strasbourg.

1951 European Coal and Steel Community (ECSC) is inaugurated by the Treaty of Paris.

1954 Germany and Italy join the WEU.

1957 Treaty of Rome establishes the European Economic Community (EEC), and the European Atomic Energy Community (Euratom) consisting of Belgium, the Netherlands, Luxembourg, Germany, France and Italy.

1961 OEEC becomes OECD, as membership broadens to include other advanced industrial nations.

1967 ECSC, EEC and Euratom merge to become the European Community (EC).

1973 Denmark, Republic of Ireland and the UK join the EC.
1981 Greece joins the EC.
1986 Portugal and Spain accede.
1987 The Single Act sets the timeframe for the launch of the Single European Market by 1993.
1990 Unification of Germany.
1992 Treaty of Maastricht creates the European Union (EU).
1995 Austria, Finland and Sweden join the EU.

The European Union is noteworthy because of its rapid development and the prosperity it has brought to its members. There can be little doubt that other groups of nations will try to emulate this pattern of success. The whole principle is one of strength through unity. Small nations can obtain access to larger markets without having to pay tariffs. The Netherlands is one example of this; with a population of 18 million, about the size of one region of Germany, in 1995 the EU accounted for more than 77% of its exports.

Large nations such as Germany have access to an even greater market, now accounting for over 350 million customers, and achieve even greater economies of scale.

Of course, not all citizens of the EU see it as a success. Some see it as representing a loss of national independence. But no sovereign state is really independent in the last decade of the twentieth century. Research shows that 90% of business people in the UK were in favour of the EU in 1997, and also that the more people understand the workings of the EU, the more they tend to be in favour of it. Of course, it is far from perfect, and there have been numerous scandals involving the misuse of European funds. But similar scandals have not been unknown in national governments in the European Union, and the EU is now exercising tighter fiscal control over its budgets.

Bureaucracy, too, has been known to get out of hand among officials of the EU. There really is a European Directive which states how curved a banana should be! But the rumour that EU fishermen must wear hair nets while on the high seas is strictly spurious.

The most important legislation of the European Union was the Single European Act. This was designed to promote the free movement throughout the Community, as it was then called, of goods, services, capital and labour. In addition, a central EU Bank and a common

Single currency set to boost travel industry

Paul Norris looks at an ABTA commissioned report which analysed who would be the winners and losers if a single European currency was introduced.

Increased holiday prices would be more than offset by the savings in exchange transactions if a single European currency is introduced, according to an ABTA-commissioned survey.

Douglas McWilliams, chief executive of the London-based Centre for Economics and Business Research which carried out the study, estimates travellers to the Continent would save £4.30 per trip in currency transactions.

But holidays would be more expensive as the UK would be forced to lower its exchange rate if it joined the European Monetary Union.

"Traditional destinations like Greece and Spain would suffer as their currencies would be higher, they would have to go more upmarket to attract customers," said McWilliams.

He estimated Spain would have 20% fewer tourists in 2010 than it has now, and budget holidays would become less common.

However, he said destinations like Turkey and Croatia, which would not be included in the first phase of the single currency, would benefit as the pound is still quite strong against their currencies.

"Countries in the southern Mediterranean, like Tunisia, would also benefit," he said.

The CEBR said the number of visits to countries outside the European Union would rise by 50%–55% and inter-EU travel would increase by 25%–35%. He said air travellers would also benefit as fares were likely to become more standard through a single banking system and savings would inevitably be passed on to passengers through agents.

European tourists visiting the UK would benefit through the dropping of EU currencies – McWilliams said a typical traveller would save £9.20 a trip.

ABTA's head of policy and member services, Stephen Alcock, said: "The CEBR believes our industry is well-placed to face the uncertainties of the Euro and winners will more than outweigh losers because of the stimulus the EMU will give to the market.

"The study is pretty positive and Douglas McWilliams was impressed with the ability of our industry in handling exchange fluctuations."

Source: Travel Weekly, 20 August 1997

currency were set as goals to be realized in the near future. In some ways the EU is imitating the USA. It would be inconceivable to have to change your currency every time you travelled from one state of the USA to another. Therefore, a single currency is the next logical stage of development of the EU. The article on page 97 discusses the effect of the single currency on the travel industry.

Chapter review

Market selection, market research and free trade associations have much in common, as they will together tend to determine which markets an organization will select and often, just as important, how it will prioritize them. It is not a coincidence that almost 65% of the EU's 'exports' go to other countries within the EU.

Questions

Section A: Class discussion

1   Analyse, with examples, the relationship between product characteristics and market selection.
2   List some trade barriers and explain to which markets they might apply.
3   What are the main problems of international marketing research?
4   What do you think a major effect of the extension of Free Trade Associations could be?
5   List the pros and cons of a single currency for the European Union.

Section B: Examination revision

1   Take a consumer product manufactured in your country. Explain how you would go about selecting suitable markets for it.
2   How can an organization make its international market research more cost-effective?
3   To what extent should intermediaries be used to carry out a firm's market research?
4   Do you think the European Union is likely to develop into a much closer unit? If so, how?

5   Do you think the percentage of exports of the EU to other countries is likely to increase over the next decade? State your reasons.

References

Cecchini, P. (1988) *The European Challenge of 1992: The Benefits of a Single Market*, Wildwood House, Aldershot.

Majaro, S. (1982) *International Market Profile Analysis*, revised edn, Allen & Unwin (Reprinted by Routledge, 1993).

6

Market entry strategy I: Options mainly used by larger firms

❏ CHAPTER PREVIEW

Companies have a wide range of possibilities for market entry strategy. However, they need to choose the right one for each market, bearing in mind the particular circumstances. In this chapter we will examine the market entry strategies more suitable for larger organizations, such as licensing, franchising and manufacture overseas.

This topic relates particularly to planning and commitment, but also to the cultural impact on international marketing.

❏ BY THE END OF THIS CHAPTER YOU SHOULD:

■ Understand the importance of market entry strategy

■ Appreciate the different options available for market entry strategy

■ Understand which options are more suitable for larger organizations

- ■ **Appreciate the advantages of licensing and franchising**
- ■ **Appreciate the advantages of assembly and manufacture overseas.** ❏

The development of international marketing in the modern world

This subject is currently one of great sophistication and complexity owing to the phenomenal development of all kinds of international commercial operations since the Second World War. Thus the student has to identify the various structures and processes of the vast and numerous international trading activities currently going on, with their significant effect on society at large.

The classification of these processes and their meaning and justification, with especial reference to the specifically import/export processes, are a major contribution to the student's progress of assimilation and subsequent professional career in this field.

The internationalization of a company

Traditionally, a firm follows a certain pattern on its road towards internationalization. It often starts with 'accidental' exporting, from overseas orders not solicited. It often then proceeds to have its own export strategy. Finally it often manufactures in different overseas countries.

To illustrate the matter, let us begin with a fictitious example of a small company which establishes a market for its goods. Because of the growth in the demand for its products, it prospers and the demand then extends to customers in other countries.

Examples of this are all around us, from exclusive products like Dom Pérignon champagne from France, Gucci leatherware from Italy or Levi Strauss jeans from the United States, all imports from other countries to the United Kingdom, and similarly Scotch whisky, Dundee marmalade or Harrier vertical take-off fighter aircraft, exported overseas from the UK.

In fact, such is the complexity of trade and commerce in the modern world that few products are now made from start to finish in one country.

Most products have raw materials or components which are produced in another country.

Let us continue, however, with our fictitious company, which finds a demand for its products abroad. If this demand is sustained it will have to appoint an individual or a department to handle the sale and dispatch of those products to their destination. This person or department, be it an export clerk, an export manager or complete export department, depending on size and degree of activity, will also have to be concerned with such matters as insurance, currency conversion, freight rates and shipping schedules as well as the overseas marketing functions.

Should the demand continue to increase in certain markets, a decision might be taken to produce partially or completely in a foreign country in order to be able to supply customers in that particular market or even in adjacent markets. Such an arrangement might avoid having to pay high tariffs – one of the motives for Nissan building its factory in northern England, as we mentioned in Chapter 1, was so that its cars could enter the European Union market.

In such a case, the decision might be to establish subsidiary companies in foreign countries, and all the administration concerning the interaction of these subsidiary companies with the head office might be through the setting up of an international division.

At such a point in its operational growth the firm may be dealing directly with its overseas subsidiary companies, and acts like a company with different operational sites, even though these are situated in different countries. Since these are essentially operations between different parts of the same company, they transcend the need for an export department as such and matters are handled by the international division.

In a number of cases these large international organizations, known as either transnational corporations or multinational corporations (MNCs), set up a headquarters operation in a different country from that of their country of origin, thereby treating their domestic factories and operations as yet another subsidiary company. This move may be made in order to obtain more favourable tax conditions, and is not the general rule for all MNCs. However, it does illustrate the point that all MNCs consider themselves global rather than national entitites, with the operations in their country of origin as just one of their many international activities.

The methods of expansion to overseas markets vary, however, because of a number of differing situations, to be discussed later, which determine whether expansion is to be by means of manufacture abroad, licensing, franchising or any number of combinations.

It is also necessary to note that companies engaged in international operations employ different methods in different countries, as conditions allow, or prove to be more effective, so there is no one correct method that fits a situation at any one time. Each situation must be judged on the prevailing conditions and decisions taken accordingly. Hence international operations, such as exporting, must be constantly under review and the methods themselves change over time and because of changing circumstances.

A good example of this would be the exporting arrangements with the former Soviet Union, where all transactions had to take place under the direction and control of a central government authority, the State Trading Corporation. With the change of political system and the reversion to a market economy in that area, all companies will now be considering alternative trading arrangements, more in line with Western economies.

Thus with international marketing and international trade the situation is never fixed and changes according to the current economic, social, political and technical as well as commercial environment. Students must learn to recognize this and it is the export practitioner's role to anticipate the changes and grasp the opportunities as they arise.

With regard to importing operations, which have not been mentioned to date, these are, of course, mirror images of the export operation. That is, every item exported by one country is received as an import by another. In this way, all the principles applying to export procedures similarly, with some few modifications, apply to import operations. All these operations therefore involve buyers and sellers, importers and exporters.

Together with the multinational operations mentioned above they form the basis of international trade and international marketing. Figure 6.1 shows market entry through foreign ventures and joint operations.

Apart from direct exporting which will be discussed in Chapter 7, there are a number of other international marketing operations, some for the purpose of entering a new market, such as licensing, and others, like contract manufacture, mainly for supporting existing operations in other markets.

Figure 6.1 Market entry through foreign ventures and joint operations

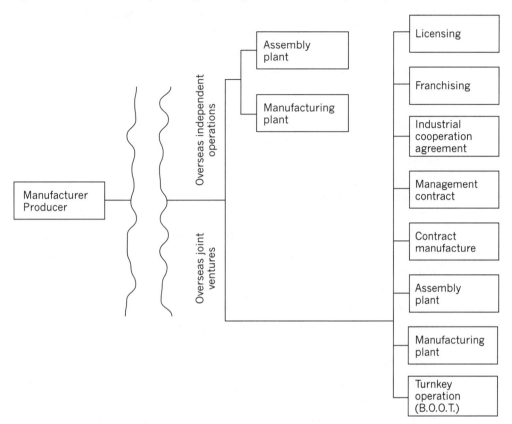

There are many options and the decision to follow one or more of these options is normally determined by existing conditions.

Licensing

The practice of manufacturing under licence, or licensing, which is given by a company with a patent or special process or technical know-how to another company in a foreign market, is one option. The former company with the patented product is the licensor who grants permission, or gives the licence, to the licensee to manufacture their product under licence.

For this type of agreement the licensor receives a commission, or royalty, on every item manufactured and sold by the licensee.

The practice of licensing rather than exporting directly into a foreign market may be from choice or due to existing circumstances.

The receipt of royalties on products sold by the licensee will be lower than a profit margin on products exported directly. However, there is the advantage that, apart from a monitoring system, there will be far fewer costs of manufacture, investment or operation. It will therefore be more advantageous to grant a licence and obtain a return in the short term rather than go to the extent of building a production plant as well as developing a market for the product. In this case there will be virtually immediate returns from this transaction.

Furthermore, in some countries, because of government policies or high tariffs, entry by licensing may be the only method. This was formerly the case with most Latin American countries. Through manufacture under licence in a foreign country the product is essentially a product made in that country, and may then qualify for admission to government tendering contracts, which is a serious consideration to be taken into account when governments have such considerable buying power. It will also be perceived as a product of that country, which may greatly help its marketing there.

In other cases licensing may be the only means of trading without extending existing manufacturing facilities in the home market. For instance Nestlé, the manufacturer of Kit-Kat chocolate bars, license their product to Hershey, the foremost chocolate manufacturer in the United States. Rowntrees (now a subsidiary of Nestlé) could not manufacture for both the British and American markets without building new manufacturing facilities, so the current arrangement is much more suitable. There is, however, a downside to the licensing process. Having granted a licence, as well as receiving a lower return, the licensor is cut off from the marketing process and cannot really gauge whether the licensee is really exploiting the market to its full potential.

Also, the licensee poses a potential threat as a competitor when the licensing agreement runs out. The only way around this problem is for the licensor to upgrade the product, so as to give it a distinct competitive edge over the last one, so that the licensee will enter into a new agreement with the updated version when the old agreement runs out.

Franchising

Similar to licensing but with its unique features, a franchise operation is to marketing what licensing is to production.

The franchisor is generally a company that supplies a service and, having gained expertise in offering that service, makes an agreement with the franchisee for that service to be offered to the public under certain recognizable features.

Examples are the Kentucky Fried Chicken chain or Dynorod pipe de-blocking services where the service is well known to the public because of its national advertising and various promotional ventures. The franchisee, usually a small entrepreneur, puts up a small amount of capital and obtains the franchise to operate within a given catchment area. This is usually by means of some initial payment and a royalty on the proceeds of the business.

The franchisor will supply distinctive logos for its sales outlets, down to the uniforms the staff wear, and also will train and direct staff to perform the service in a distinctive way. Backed by national advertising campaigns which would be out of the reach of such a small business, the franchisee obtains the benefit of this promotion. In turn, the franchisor does not have to set up its own marketing chain but relies upon the many franchisees. There is also the additional benefit of providing raw materials, logos, uniforms, services, etc. to the franchisee, which are produced in bulk, therefore incurring economies of scale and thus serving to increase the profitablity of the franchisor's operation. In return the franchisee agrees to be closely monitored by the franchisor. Franchisees are usually quite happy to agree to this, in order to maintain the reputation of the brand name.

Assembly and manufacture overseas

As mentioned in Chapter 1, international marketing and multinational operations can include the manufacture of complete products or component parts in various parts of the world. There are a number of reasons for this, for instance the proximity of the source of supply to the market, rendering a faster and more efficient service to consumers, or the lower costs of land, labour or capital, which can give the operation a competitive advantage.

In many instances, companies are offered advantageous terms by host governments, who see such moves as the answer to problems of local unemployment. Examples of this are the British government's endeavours to attract manufacturing to the north of England or Northern Ireland.

Inducements such as tax 'holidays,' or purpose-built infrastructures (transport and communications), training facilities for employees and land grants are all part of the packages that governments offer companies to set up manufacturing and assembly plants in their countries.

Contract manufacture

In this case the company give a contract to a company based in the target market to manufacture some of its products. Although the objective is the same as providing foreign-made products rather than exporting them from the country of origin, the manufacturing is done by an independent company. This saves the international organization the costs of building factories for the manufacture of their products and relies upon existing local production facilities.

There is obviously an advantage to this course of action. Production and administrative costs will be minimized but it depends totally upon whether suitable facilities or experienced management and labour exist. The degree of quality and the problems which this can create mean that control needs to be considered when undertaking such an agreement.

Industrial cooperation agreement

These agreements, which may vary in scope, essentially are ideal for companies in two countries to cooperate in manufacturing know-how or research and development. They will allow for the sharing of costs of research and development and of manufacturing processes, where both parties stand to gain from such cooperation (see Figure 6.1).

It seems paradoxical that they bring together rival companies to cooperate. However, because this type of agreement involves large companies which are too big to be absorbed by their rival, the agreement, where each party obtains the benefit from the pooled results of technological development, is considered mutually beneficial.

Many of the organizations involved in this type of venture are electrical companies, like the agreement between electronic manufacturers such as Philips and Sony, and computer companies as exemplified by the agreement between ICL and Fujitsu.

Takeovers

These became a particularly popular way in the 1980s of acquiring the know-how of a market, expertise in manufacturing and/or leading brands. While it may seem an expensive form of market entry strategy, and it usually is to begin with, very often the investment pays off handsomely in the long run. Two firms which have used this strategy consistently and successfully are Nestlé and Electrolux.

Management contracts

These are agreements between the owners of a large and complex operation, which may be a holding company and only interested in the results, and an expert group accustomed to managing such a type of organization. The managers will then run the organization at a profit for the benefit of the owners on a remuneration basis.

This type of agreement seems to apply particularly to the hotel industry where Hilton, Sheraton and Holiday Inn hotels are run according to such a contract. The managers of such hotel complexes have developed a fine expertise and run the business on behalf of the various owners in different countries.

These contracts also apply in similar types of organization such as hospitals. In these cases the owners are state governments, in such places as the Middle East, where the supply of trained personnel is limited and they require experienced administrators, medical, nursing and technical staff to run the hospitals efficiently.

Recently there have been instances of tenders for street cleansing put out by local government in the UK, where the contract was awarded to a French company with expertise in the efficient running of such operations.

Turnkey operations

Perhaps these agreements should be considered a mixture of some of the above. They concern large construction projects such as oil refineries, oil terminals, hospitals and airports where the supply of products is varied and there is also a large element of human resources and skills involved.

The suppliers of the total product, usually a consulting and management organization, undertake to bring all the different plant and machinery to the site of the project, at the same time arranging for the training of the personnel who will run the project on its completion.

At a prearranged date the delivery of the plant is made to the owners and the 'key' for the running of the plant is handed over to them, the inference being that with the turning of the key everything within the plant will start to function. Power will flow, wheels will turn and personnel will supervise the operation from that moment. However, in practice, a consultancy agreement is often built in, which means that the supplier may have engineers working at the new plant for at least a year.

Some suppliers of public utilities, such as power stations or water purification plants, negotiate agreements with governments of Third World nations to build and operate an installation. In some cases the suppliers will build and operate the plant for a set period, during which they will recover their costs and profits and then transfer ownership to the national government. These are known as BOOT operations (Build, Operate, Own and Transfer) or any variations of the above.

As an international trading operation it indicates a combination of many skills, technical, managerial and commercial, which are channelled through the main supplier for the successful conclusion of the project.

Barter, countertrading and buy-back

This chapter would not be complete without a mention of this form of trading, which affects all of the above, and can feature largely in the negotiation stages of the contract.

Countries with a lack of hard currency but with large resources of a particular raw material may want to pay partially or totally in materials rather than in currency, or to barter or set up some form of countertrading arrangement with the suppliers.

This may involve a third party, who either purchases the raw material from the buyer and pays the seller an agreed price, or contracts to find one or more purchasers for the raw material.

Another form of countertrade is buy-back, whereby the seller of a particular product, such as plant or machinery, will agree, as part of the deal, to accept some of the products made by that machinery in the country of the purchaser as part payment. For example, Wilkinson Sword built a razor blade plant in the former Soviet Union and took back a portion of the blades produced by the Russian factory as part of the payment, for sale elsewhere.

Another form of this kind of arrangement, usually in dealings between governments for such items as military equipment, but not necessarily so, is offset trading, where the agreement to purchase a product is dependent upon the seller's country agreeing to buy material equivalent to the total or partial price of the contract.

Chapter review

This is a vital area in international marketing. A firm has many possibilities, but must try to find the most appropriate one for each market, bearing in mind the control it will give and the investment which is required, both in finance and in management skills.

Questions

Section A: Class discussion

1 Give some reasons for opting for creating a manufacturing facility in a market as a market entry strategy.
2 Discuss the problems and advantages of international takeovers.
3 Explain some problems caused by market entry barriers and how these could be overcome by an appropriate market entry strategy.
4 Discuss some of the advantages of a joint venture.
5 What is the paradox of international cooperation agreements and why are they considered? Give some real or fictitious examples to support your answer.

Section B: Examination revision

1 How important is control of the marketing in a target market, and what options give the organization the most control?

2   Do you see any relationship between the amount of investment and the amount of control in an overseas market?
3   Examine the main advantages and drawbacks of licensing, quoting examples of each.
4   What are the advantages and problems for the buyer of a turnkey operation?
5   Choosing an industrial product, examine the question of market entry strategy, and suggest some appropriate strategies for a specific market.

References

Bradley, F. (1991) *International Marketing Strategy*, Chapter 9, Prentice-Hall.

Young, S., Hamill, J., Wheeler, C. and Richard Davies, J. (1989) *International Market Entry and Development – Strategies and Management*, Harvester Wheatsheaf – Prentice-Hall.

7

Market entry strategy II: Options mainly used by smaller organizations

Smaller firms often cannot use some of the market entry strategies mentioned in the last chapter, particularly takeovers and joint ventures. The most popular market entry strategies for them are using agents and distributors, although some of them set up their own marketing subsidiary in one market.

This topic relates very closely to the preceding chapter but these market entry strategies will be used in the main by SMEs. However, some of these options may also be used by larger organizations for some markets.

❏   BY THE END OF THIS CHAPTER YOU SHOULD:

■   Be aware of the role of export houses and confirming houses

■   Understand the importance of the selection of the right mode of market entry strategy for the smaller firm

■   Understand the different roles of agent and distributor

- **Be aware of when each might be appropriate**
- **Be aware of the potential of wholly owned marketing subsidiary in the target country**
- **Be aware of the market research needed in the selection of an intermediary.** ❑

Indirect exporting

Indirect exporting is the selling of goods in one country to a buyer who then undertakes to transport them to another country (Figure 7.1).

At a very simple level, a tourist seeing an item in a shop window and

Figure 7.1 Indirect export operations

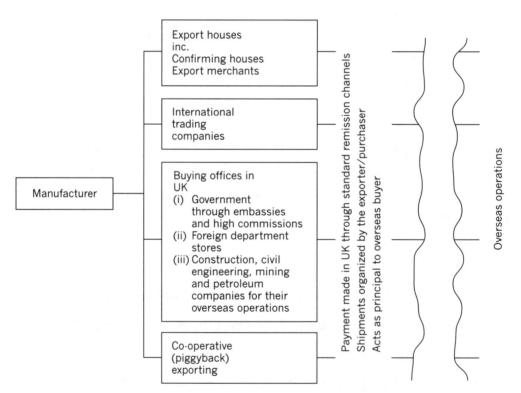

buying it to take home is in fact undertaking indirect exporting. The costs of transportation, however minimal, are borne by this tourist, as are the declaration of the item at the customs and the payment of duty at the tourist's destination. Also, payment will be made on the spot, by the tourist at the point of purchase.

A commercial parallel to this is the individual purchaser of a machine or other piece of equipment exhibited on a stand at a trade fair, who negotiates a price for the item and then arranges for its transportation overseas.

In international transactions there are a number of similar instances but on a larger and more complex scale. There are various types of organizations that cater for this type of business and they will all be discussed in turn.

Manufacturers can therefore engage in indirect exporting without necessarily equipping themselves for overseas operations. The disadvantage in this case, however, is that it is very passive and relies upon the efforts of another party. Also, the producer is denied access to the final user of the product and thus cannot ascertain how suitable it was for that market. In addition, the intermediary is likely to be earning the major part of the profits.

Nevertheless, indirect exporting is very popular in some industries and does not mean that direct exporting is precluded, although there can be instances where complications may arise as will be discussed later. But as it is an important aspect of international trade it requires serious investigation.

Major overseas buyers are very frequently foreign governments. With regard to military equipment as well as equipment for schools, hospitals, railways, communications and many other goods, governments are always on the lookout for products which may update their existing resources in these areas.

Such purchasing is usually done through the embassies (and High Commissions of Commonwealth nations in the UK) who will contact manufacturers of the products they are interested in and possibly commence the negotiations. Depending upon the extent of the contract, these negotiations may extend to the buyer's country.

Other organizations which specialize in this kind of business are export merchants. These are companies which have business contacts in foreign countries and specialize in obtaining goods for their clients.

These merchant companies generally either specialize in a particular group of products such as food or textiles, or alternatively represent clients in a specific geographic region like West Africa or South America (see Figure 7.1).

Confirming houses

Confirming houses are similar to the above and carry out very comparable functions.

These companies also undertake to seek appropriate products on behalf of their clients overseas but there is a financial element involved, so that as well as supplying the product they finance their clients' operation.

Corporate UK buying offices

Many large department stores have buying offices in the UK seeking products suitable for export to stand on their shelves. Products like Scottish salmon, marmalade and goods of that nature are in demand by shoppers at large European and Japanese stores so that the buyers can see the products at first hand and negotiate accordingly.

Also, many large construction and petroleum companies buy equipment in the UK to send out to their various operations overseas.

International trading companies

These are large trading organizations established in different parts of the world such as the United Africa Company in West Africa or Burns Philp in Australasia, which run trading posts and stores in various parts of their market. Like the UK buying offices above, they purchase goods in the UK and elsewhere to supply their stores.

In all such cases the buyer, in the UK, pays for the goods in sterling from an existing account in the UK and undertakes the transportation of the goods and payment of duties at their destination.

Direct exporting

Where the seller of the goods contacts and negotiates with a buyer in a foreign country, and undertakes the risks of delivery and receipt of payment, this can be considered direct exporting (Figure 7.2).

This definition can be modified somewhat by the fact that negotiation can be done via a third party, an agent.

Figure 7.2 Direct export operations

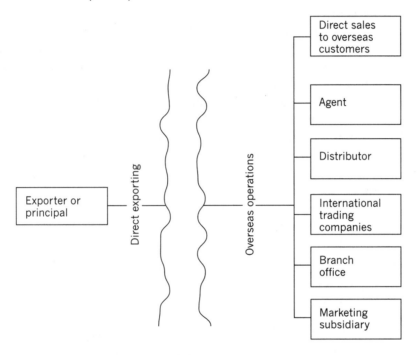

For very exclusive products, aircraft, specialized machinery or works of art, it might be possible for a seller to travel to the customer's country and meet the customer face-to-face for a direct sale – a perfect example of direct exporting. However, this type of contract is relatively rare. Even with such products as exemplified above, there is usually a party, like an agent, who learns of the demand and puts the buyer and seller in contact, or even undertakes negotiations on behalf of the exporter or principal.

The export agent

Most exporters, unless conducting their own operations, make use of an export agent. Due to the lack of fluency in foreign languages, this is a particularly popular strategy for British exporters. The agent is a legal entity, an individual or a company, who undertakes to act on behalf of an exporter, in this case known as the principal, who is the supplier or manufacturer of the goods.

By definition an agent never has title to the goods. Ownership of the goods rests with the principal until they are sold to the customer or importer. That does not mean that the agent cannot handle or keep the goods. As we shall see, there are agents who keep consignment stocks on behalf of their principals. However, an agent does not own the goods but sells them on a commission basis.

The usefulness of agents lies in the fact that they are resident in the importing country and that they are accustomed to the marketplace, know about the ways of doing business in that market, get to learn about the level of demand and business activity and, of course, since they are mostly nationals of that country, are fluent in the local language and idioms.

There are three types of agents:

- Exclusive agents
- Consignment agents
- Del credere agents

This is not a mutually exclusive list; being one type does not exclude the possibility of being another. It is the nature of their function that counts.

- The exclusive agent, as the name implies, has exclusive rights to operate in a particular territory. The principal will not appoint another agent in the same part of the country and any business obtained, whether directly by the agent or dealt with by the principal, has to carry a commission for the agent. This is because it is assumed that a customer within that territory buying the product, whether from the agent or directly from the principal, will have done so as a result of the agent's promotion and activity within that territory.

Within the European Union, where an exclusive agent may be seen by the Commission to act against the freedom of the customer to choose products from the best source possible, the agent has to prove that acting exclusively would be in the best interests of the consumer. That is, because of the agent's expertise in handling or servicing the product.

● The consignment agent is allowed by the principal to keep a consignment stock of goods, components or spare parts, so that rapid service can be offered to customers.

● The del credere agent has a special function. As well as negotiating a sale, this type of agent has a responsibility for making good bad debts from their customers.

There are certain implications in this procedure. One is that the agent will be wary about with whom he decides to deal, since a poor payer will mean a loss for him, rather than for the principal. Another is that this type of agent will require a higher commission because of the additional risk.

The whole question of the appointment and use of export agents is one which requires further attention and this matter will be dealt with in the next section.

The distributor

An alternative to using an agent is to appoint a distributor, which is an individual or a company who purchases goods on their own behalf. The role the distributor plays is similar to that of an agent, that is, to sell the goods to customers. However, the difference is that the distributor is the owner of the goods and resells them to his or her customers with a mark-up instead of commission.

Having invested in the product there is greater motivation by the distributor to obtain a return on that investment, hence the preference for a distributor over an agent. However, because of the product being owned by the distributor there is a possibility that too great a mark-up may be attached, reducing the volume of sales.

Principals should also be wary of distributors of products, such as machinery, who simply wish to use it in their own business. In this way the distributor is not really exploiting the market but pretending to do so while buying a product at a reduced price for his or her own use.

Both distributors and agents are independent organizations who work for a number of principals. In this case they do not devote all of their working time to one principal and the exporter should be aware of that and try as much as possible to motivate them to market their products rather than those of another principal.

Branch office

Because of the problems of controlling agents and distributors and monitoring the market, frequent visits need to be made and the exporter's presence should be felt in that country. However, the geographical distance may render this difficult to implement.

One way to make this practical would be to establish a branch office, either in one foreign country for handling that particular market, or in the centre of a group of adjacent countries for covering a certain area, such as South East Asia or the Middle East.

The office would be staffed by people employed by the principal which means they would be working continuously for that one company. Their job would be to visit the nearby agents and distributors frequently and deal with problems on the spot. An extension of this would be to have service and stocking facilities at the branch.

This would seem to be a kind of halfway house to establishing a subsidiary company in a host country, putting the operation completely in the control of the parent company.

Subsidiary company

Where there is sufficient demand and as illustrated by the Chart in Fig. 7.2, the company may invest in setting up both a manufacturing and marketing operation in a foreign country. The degree of investment, that is, either a wholly or partially owned subsidiary, depends upon the amount of financial resources available locally or even upon legal constraints. Some countries forbid a controlling interest in any national company, with a stipulated maximum foreign holding of 49%.

At this stage of development, as mentioned above, the process really ceases to be classified as an export operation and the various overseas subsidiaries work in conjunction with the head office, very much like departments of an organization. Products are not exported as such, but transferred from one part of the multinational organization to the other with some form of internal costing procedure to account for the transaction.

The mainstay of the international marketing process for many companies, therefore, is the appointment and control of agents, and the remainder of this chapter is devoted to this matter.

The role and function of export agents

As mentioned above, agents are one of the most popular forms of exporting channels for British exporters. This was confirmed in a report some years ago produced by a team from UMIST (University of Manchester Institute of Science and Techology. Turnbull & Cunningham)

Apart from being a low cost operation, the popularity of this strategy stemmed from the fact that it overcame the language problem. The inability to negotiate in a foreign language forced companies into using agents for that purpose. The report criticized this trend since the use of agents rather than company executives was less effective.

Agents, as mentioned before, may serve a number of principals and there is a danger here that they may either neglect one principal at the expense of another or alternatively handle competitive material.

In developing countries, agents usually handle a vast number of different products, from automotive parts to foodstuffs. As the markets grow more sophisticated, a rationalization takes place and it is this factor that an exporter should look for when selecting an agent.

Ideally the agent should handle complementary products, thus achieving great cost-saving in travel time which is frequently a major expense. In addition, the agent may already have entrée to a special buyer, and this is not easy to obtain. For example, automotive equipment would go with car batteries and radio equipment would go with alarm systems.

The following is a list of marketing functions which should be shared between the principal and the agent and should provide the basis for a good working arrangement:

● The prospecting and maintaining of contacts within the country
● Negotiation and face-to-face selling

- Pricing (i.e. the setting of an appropriate price for that market)
- Credit provision (where appropriate)
- Stock holding
- Physical distribution
- After-sales service and handling of complaints
- Adaptation of the product and/or the package to the needs of the market (agent to advise accordingly)
- Market research, feedback information and market intelligence
- Promotion and promotional material, dissemination of information to customers
- Coordination of marketing and strategic decisions
  (Adapted from Duguid and Jacques, *Case Studies in Export Organisation*, HMSO, 1975)

Another list of mutual obligations and duties is advised by the Institute of Export:

Duties of the agent

(a)   To take all reasonable care in handling of the principal's business
(b)   To report back all information
(c)   Not to accept bribes (from, say, competitors' agents) or obtain a secret profit (by selling at a higher price)
(d)   Not to reveal confidential information
(e)   To be accountable to the principal

In their turn the principals have their set of duties and obligations:

Duties of the principal

(a)   To pay commission on goods sold
(b)   To pay the agent's expenses (if part of the agreement)
(c)   To pay commission on orders emanating from the agent's territory but not sent in by the agent
(d)   The treatment of repeat orders (same as above, commission must be paid to the agent even though the order came direct from the customer)
(e)   Principal to reserve discretion on accepting orders from the agent's territory (i.e. the right to refuse to supply)

Note: items (c) and (d) are very important. Agents have a right to demand commission on all products sold in their territory even though they do not process them themselves. The sale may have been the result of previous efforts. That is why the principal should reserve commission on a sale even if there is no agent in the territory. In the event of an agent eventually being appointed and a repeat order being received from a customer, the agent will demand commission on it. The customer will expect to pay the same price and unless commission is reserved the principal will make a loss.

Item (e) means that an agent may have to forgo a sale and its resulting commission if the principal refuses to accept it, say because of a poor payment record. However, the principal should take care not to violate the EU's rules on restriction to trade in such instances.

Agency agreements

Both the Institute of Export of the United Kingdom and the International Chamber of Commerce set out models for draft agreements between principals and agents. Other countries have similar bodies which undertake this role. These usually make provision for such clauses as the nature of the job, the territory to be covered and the amount of support to be expected. Important changes took place in these rules for EU member states in January 1994, which all firms should be aware of.

Also of importance would be the duration of the contract and the terms of termination of the agreement. Lastly, in this very brief coverage, the law which will apply for the drafting of the agreement, whether that of the principal's or the agent's country. This is a factor of major consideration in case of a dispute.

Search for and selection of agents

The following list is not exclusive and not in order of importance. The items are ones which are recommended as being the most appropriate but further steps might be necessary in cases where a suitable agent has not been located.

Banks (usually have a working relationship with their corresponding
    banks overseas)
Chambers of Commerce
Department of Trade and Industry (which has a Commercial Officer

active in every embassy and consulate throughout the world) or
similar government department

Personal visit to the market (can learn a lot from this method)

Participation in a trade mission (organized by the DTI or similar government department and trade associations)

Taking a stand at an international trade fair

Recommendations from other principals (of complementary products)

Recommendations from members of the local business community

Approaches from prospective agents

Agent's background

In the event of an agent being located, certain investigations should be
made:

Economic and financial status (status reports can be obtained from
banks, the DTI or similar government department, and companies
like Dun and Bradstreet, who specialize in this)

Other principals (who may have heard of or dealt with that agent)

Other products handled (if complementary or competitive)

Local reputation (may require a visit to the market for this)

Size of salesforce (or one-man band)

Stocking/warehousing facilities

Servicing facilities/technical knowledge

(All the above apply also for distributors – plus a negotiated initial
consignment of stock.)

The European Community's rules on competition

As mentioned in the last chapter, the appointment of an exclusive agent
in any of the European Community countries may run counter to
Articles 85 and 86 of the Treaty of Rome.

The EU wants to prevent any form of agreement which prevents the
free forces of the marketplace from acting, so restricting people from
outside an agent's territory from ordering from that agent (perhaps
because he or she is more efficient than the agent nearest to them) is
illegal.

However, there are situations when an agency can make a case for
'negative clearance' or 'block exemption' from this restraint if they can
prove to the Commission that by acting exclusively they are doing so in

the customer's best interests. For instance, they could offer better service facilities or they have more experience of handling a complex product.

Control

The main aim of the principal is to gain maximum control over its markets. In general terms, the greater the control, the greater the level of investment needed. A wholly owned subsidiary in the target market, for example, will need much more investment than appointing an agent. However, the former offers much better long-term potential.

Chapter review

This chapter examined market entry strategies which are mainly associated with smaller companies, especially the use of an agent or distributor in the market. It is essential to know which is the most appropriate and to carry out careful market research before taking the important decision of selecting one.

Questions

Section A: Class discussion

1 Why are fewer firms today using export houses and confirming houses to do business internationally?
2 What are the main problems involved in direct exporting?
3 Why do SMEs often use agents?
4 Briefly explain the difference between a distributor and an agent and in what circumstances you would appoint each.
5 What problems may arise when an organization appoints an agent who represents several principals?

Section B: Examination revision

1 What are the pros and cons of appointing an agent rather than a distributor? Do some firms use both methods of market entry, in different markets?

2 In what circumstances might using a confirming house be the best option?

3 As a consultant, in what circumstances would you advise your client to set up its own marketing subsidiary in a market?

4 What precautions should a firm take before appointing an agent based in an EU country?

5 What precautions should a firm take before appointing a distributor to a market with considerable potential?

References

Schmittoff, C. (1990) The Export Trade 9th Edition, Stevens and Co.

Walker, A.G. (1995) International Trade Procedures and Management, Butterworth-Heinemann.

Young, S., Hamill, J., Wheeler, C. and Richard Davies, J. (1989) *International Market Entry and Development – Strategies and Management*, Harvester Wheatsheaf – Prentice-Hall.

8

Product strategy

❏   CHAPTER PREVIEW

The product we are marketing is obviously one of the most important aspects of international marketing. However, the concept of
product in international marketing needs different emphasis for
different types of product, as we will show. For this reason we
need to consider the product in every area of the subject. The
type of product we are marketing is going to have a profound
influence on all other issues, from considerations of the environment for international marketing, through long-term planning and
commitment, to communications with the market, the impact of
culture and market entry strategy. We cannot ignore the product
when considering any aspect of international marketing, as its
influence is everywhere.

Closely related areas are long-term planning and commitment,
market selection strategy, communications with the market and
market entry.

❏   BY THE END OF THIS CHAPTER YOU SHOULD:

■   Be aware of the complexity of the total product concept in the
    field of international marketing

■ Be able to understand the concepts of generic, expected, augmented and potential product and how they may be applied and their relevance in an international marketing context

■ Understand the concept of competitive advantage and how it applies to certain industries

■ Understand the potential advantages of globalization and the constraints it can have in international marketing

■ Understand how product modification can be effectively implemented

■ Understand how 'intangible' may be a relative term in an international marketing context.   ❑

Introduction

Product strategy is one of the most important aspects of international marketing, but also a difficult one since both strategical and tactical considerations must be made.

We need to ask ourselves what business we are in, and the answers to this question must take a long-term view. We must often view the company and its service from the point of view of our customers and other stakeholders, and ask ourselves what products they will want in ten years' time and what ecological demands they will place on us as a company. By then there may well be new technologies which will satisfy the customers' needs and wants in quite novel ways.

So, we need to ask many questions such as:

A1   Where is our market now?
A2   Where is it going?
A3   How do we get where it is going?

A4   What are the trends in our customers' markets in the case of organizational marketing?

A5   How can we expand our market?

B1   What marketing objectives do we need?

B2   What are our overall marketing strategies?

B3   Have the four major categories of strategy been investigated – market penetration, market development, product development and diversification?

C1   Is the market changing in size, structure, location or nature?

C2   Are there gaps in the market to be exploited?

C3   What are the competitors' activities and strategies?

C4   What is the market map of this market?

We will now examine some of the foregoing questions. We would suggest that you try to find the answers to the others for yourself.

   Section A   It would be futile to attempt to answer these questions in a vacuum, so we will take an example, and we suggest that you do, too. The example we shall take is a small airline with a short history such as Easyjet, which is based at London Luton Airport and offers a no-frills service at very keen prices, at present mainly for tourists.

1   Mainly tourists but with some business travellers.

2   We aim to increase the number of business travellers using our service as this represents a potential for higher profit margins.

3   We need to emphasize and increase our customer care concept.

4   Convenience of reaching the airport; at present we have an advantage over Heathrow and the traffic jams on the M25 motorway; how can we exploit this and keep this competitive advantage?

5   Consider expanding our routes, but concentrate on giving the customer what he wants.

Tactical considerations of product strategy

Product strategy is one of the most important aspects of international marketing. It concerns the total product concept, which we will explain in this chapter. The strategy we generate depends to a large extent on the product and its characteristics. A component for washing machines is likely to require a very different product strategy from lollipops. However, it is also greatly influenced by the manufacturing process involved, and the size and structure of the organization. In some cases the manufacturing process is highly flexible, giving the supplier the possibility of many different variations of the product, without substantially adding to its cost. The size of the firm is likely to determine its ability to invest in more sophisticated modes of market entry strategy, as we have already seen, such as manufacture in the target market, or setting up a wholly owned marketing subsidiary there. Both of these options give an organization a large degree of control over the marketing of their product in the overseas market. The structure of the firm plays an important role, too. A firm which belongs to a conglomerate may be able to exploit its synergy, by using the international marketing expertise already acquired by other firms in the group. This expertise could consist of special knowledge of markets, experience of organizing stands at international exhibitions, or knowledge of using channels of distribution in different markets. We will discuss the product first, and then go on to separate these concepts. We will return to this topic later.

We also examined the product concept in Chapter 3 when we discussed the findings of Turnbull and Cunningham and the importance of commercial and technical competence. We examined the way buyers look at products and saw that aspects which might seem intangible to a theorist are very real to a professional buyer. Any professional buyer will tell you that flexible delivery, joint product development and handling of complaints are very much at the core of what he or she buys. They are not optional extras.

One of the most popular European textbooks on marketing (Dibb, Symkin, Pride and Ferrell) defines the product as 'everything both favourable and unfavourable which one receives in an exchange'. It is a complexity of tangible and intangible attributes, including functional, social, and psychological utilities and benefits.

Levitt's theory of total product concept

One of T. Levitt's theories refers to the total product concept. This consists of four different categories:

Generic product
Expected product

Augmented product
Potential product

These constitute a dynamic model, one that is constantly changing, and as the level of service changes, so also do customers' expectations. If therefore we take food retailing as an example, supermarkets of ten years' ago would mainly fall into the generic product category. Ten years ago supermarkets did not show the same customer care that they do today. So generic would mean the basic store with no special facilities. The expected product of today would represent, in a supermarket, one which was well located geographically, providing plenty of parking space and with a good layout of the goods inside the store.

However, the situation is not so simple in international marketing, where even when we are marketing relatively simple products such as components, the buyer will attach great importance to integrated and punctual delivery, joint product development and consistent quality of the product.

Globalization

The next area we will examine is the theory of globalization. Unfortunately, few marketers who back this theory define what they mean by it. Globally literally means worldwide, i.e. marketing it equally to all 190 sovereign states on this planet. However, since the GNP per capita of different nations varies from $10,000 to $25,000 for the top 20 richest nations to $300 to $1000 for the bottom 40 countries, it is difficult to think of a product which could be marketed in the same form and price in every single one. We must assume from the overall tenor of the arguments in favour of global marketing that these marketers are referring basically to the world's elite countries from a point of view of wealth, e.g. the OECD countries. A car such as the Mondeo could be marketed with success in the world's richest countries. This is far from marketing it globally.

How many products which are vaunted to be global really are equally relevant to different kinds of markets? Cola drinks, it is recognized, will have different degrees of sweetness for different markets: the UK is much more sweet-toothed than France; the Germans and Swedes tend to have a much greater resistance to E numbers in food colouring than most

European countries. Marlboro cigarettes sold in France do not have the same flavour as those sold in Germany.

Figure 8.1 shows the product attributes of the generic, expected and augmented product. At the centre are the intrinsic characteristics, such as composition of the product, quality and design. These are certainly important qualities, but no professional buyer could afford to give them precedence over factors which might seem at first sight to be external characteristics or even intangible ones. In the case of certain products, particularly expensive perfumes and toiletries, the image is practically everything. Therefore the packaging, wrapping and labelling play a decisive role in the buying decision. So the packaging must be not

Figure 8.1 Product attributes in the augmented product after Levitt's total product concept

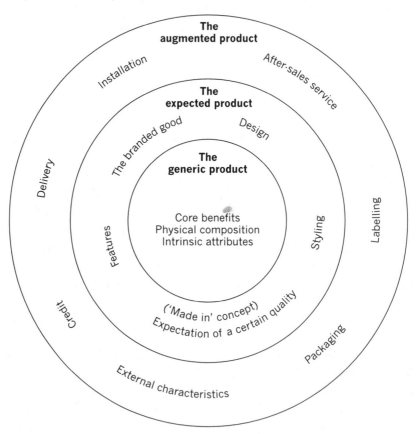

only impressive – since it appears on TV it must be also photogenic! But even more important may be the name. What we call the image will constitute an important part of the product both for the consumer and for the buyer, who in the case of perfumes are often different. So products which are often bought as gifts for other people require different promotional strategies. We can see that in a case like perfume the expression 'intrinsic qualities' has little meaning. The perception and image are all-important in international marketing.

All this is particularly relevant when we consider that many people in the EU make their buying decisions about Christmas gifts such as perfume from the TV advertisements they see. This concentrated TV advertising before Christmas is a challenge to international marketers. First of all, what viewers will be seeing is the package, because you cannot yet smell things through your TV set. The idea behind this is that when you see the same package in the shop, you will be persuaded to buy it, because you will associate it with the attractive TV advertisement. Research shows that in television advertising, in order to obtain maximum effect, you need to show the name of the product both in spoken and written form, as well as an image of the product. In the case of perfume it will be the packet – since it appears on TV it must be also photogenic.

The larger perfume companies spend a lot of money each Christmas competing against each other, because they know that Christmas is the major buying season for perfume. However, not all countries have the same laws or customs with regard to TV advertising. In some countries such as Germany, most advertising on their national channels is in blocks of 20 minutes or half an hour. This is to prevent viewers being annoyed by interruptions in their programme every few minutes, which can be the case on some German channels. However, this variation in TV legislation has a serious impact on firms needing to use TV as a medium to advertise its products. This makes the situation very different. What promotion do you think perfume companies use instead of television advertising? It is interesting to note that Germany has a much wider variety of family illustrated magazines than many other countries. These are often used to promote products advertised on TV in other markets.

Let us now take quite a different example, an industrial product, such as a sparking plug, and see if we regard this product differently. This is classed as an industrial component, and the vast majority of these are sold direct from the supplier to OEMs (original equipment manufacturers) such as Volkswagen or Renault. As we have seen in Chapter 3 on communications with the market, the physical product itself will not be the only concern of industrial buyers. They will be very much interested in the ability of the supplier to deliver the product on time and in the consistent quality of the product.

Certain markets such as Sweden, Denmark and Germany have a high awareness of environmental green factors. In some cases, as in that of Germany, the law prohibits the use of certain non-biodegradable products which were once commonly used in packing and packaging. In other cases such as the Netherlands, consumer pressure has caused environmentally unfriendly packaging not to be acceptable to supermarkets and other outlets, and manufacturers targeting that country need to substitute more environmentally friendly materials.

In the case of industrial products, fit or match with the specific market may be of paramount importance. This can vary from a compatible type of paper for use in copying or other machines, to a compatible type of electrical plug which conforms to the laws of that specific market.

In some countries such as France the tax payable on cars varies with the cubic capacity of the engine, so this must be considered when targeting certain markets with specific models of cars. As a result, different sizes of engines may be made available for certain markets such as the French one.

Different consumer markets are looking for different characteristics. Most European countries have a high demand for low temperature domestic washing machines. The UK market is an exception to this. However, if consumers in the UK become aware that lower temperature washing machines are available in other markets, the trend could change in the UK.

Design and quality are the most important unique selling propositions in many markets and this holds true for both consumer and industrial goods. Design does not simply refer to the outward appearance of the product, but also to its flexibility and general suitability for use.

We have shown that product is much more complex than it seems at first sight. These complications are increased by the perceived distance of the supplier in an international marketing context, and the need for the marketer to prove his or her credibility to the customer. The buyer needs to have a high degree of confidence in the product and the supplier he is dealing with. He therefore needs detailed information not only about the product, but about the capability of the supplier to deliver the product when required. This is one of the reasons, as we will see in Chapter 9 on promotional strategy in international marketing, why personal selling plays such an important role internationally.

Branding

The popularity of baked beans in a sweet tomato sauce is notorious with visitors to the UK even though most UK consumers do not realize that this 'typically British' dish is grown exclusively in the USA, and that baked beans are not nearly as popular in the UK as in the US.

Until the early 1990s the British baked bean market was dominated by a brand called Heinz. Such was its market share that for some years it used the message 'Beanz Meanz Heinz' in its advertising.

During the 1970s and 1980s an accelerating change took place in the food retailing industry in Western Europe. The balance of power shifted from the food manufacturer to the food retailer. What were the main causes of this? Gradually the small independent grocer was being replaced by chains of supermarkets. These organizations had enormous buying power, and could decide which brands they stocked and how much, and quote prices with which the small grocery stores could not compete. In addition, laws in many countries started to prohibit the manufacturer from forcing particular retail prices on the retailer. The expansion of the use of the car for shopping, and the provision of free parking in these hypermarkets, most of which were out of town, only served to accelerate this trend. Motorists no longer wanted to sit in long inner-city traffic jams in order to do their shopping. One logical outcome of the rise of supermarkets throughout Europe was the development of retailers' own brands which competed head-on with manufacturers' brands but often at a much lower price.

Launch of new products in overseas markets

Given the numerous variables mentioned so far in this chapter, the international marketer is faced with many factors – some of which even conflict with one another – when deciding upon the launch of a product in an overseas market.

Branding: The can of Heinz Baked Beans

'Building a brand is a long slow process and to try to take brand share away from a dominant brand is a very long and very expensive proposition, indeed in the modern retailing world it would not be attempted. So he who has holds, and that is why brands are so valuable' Tony O'Reilly, ex-president of Heinz.

For this reason Heinz has maintained brand share even through its price effectiveness against own brands has been eroded.

Branding is what has literally made the fortune of many firms. Levi Jeans is one of these. Experts admit that there is little physical difference between Levi jeans and other brands, yet customers are prepared to pay up to 40% more for a pair of Levis. This is because of the very high profile of this particular brand which is still the top seller in the world. However, it is not there by accident or by right. Levis have to work hard at maintaining this image and the high profile. Throwing money at the problem alone is not the answer. The answer is in smart advertising rather than hard advertising. Advertisements which appeal to the emotions and make the product seem 'sexy' are what sell jeans, not advertisements which simply highlight the quality of the garment. They are not selling garments, they are selling images, they are selling dreams.

In order to assist the marketer and rationalize the decision-making process, the use of a model may serve to indicate appropriate products for particular markets. This is provided for by the demonstration of the matrix originally conceived by Simon Majaro in his book *International Market Profile Analysis: A strategic approach to world markets* (revised edition published by Routledge, 1993).

Majaro adopted a matrix, which he called a Market Profile Analysis, consisting of the major elements of the marketing mix set against various environmental variables. He extended the marketing mix to five elements and set these at the top of the matrix. Each element would then be considered appropriately against certain characteristics and environmental variables of the market, as shown in Figure 8.2.

As is always the case in the study of marketing, no one element of the marketing mix stands in isolation. All aspects of marketing interrelate

Figure 8.2 Majaro's *International Market Profile Analysis* Matrix

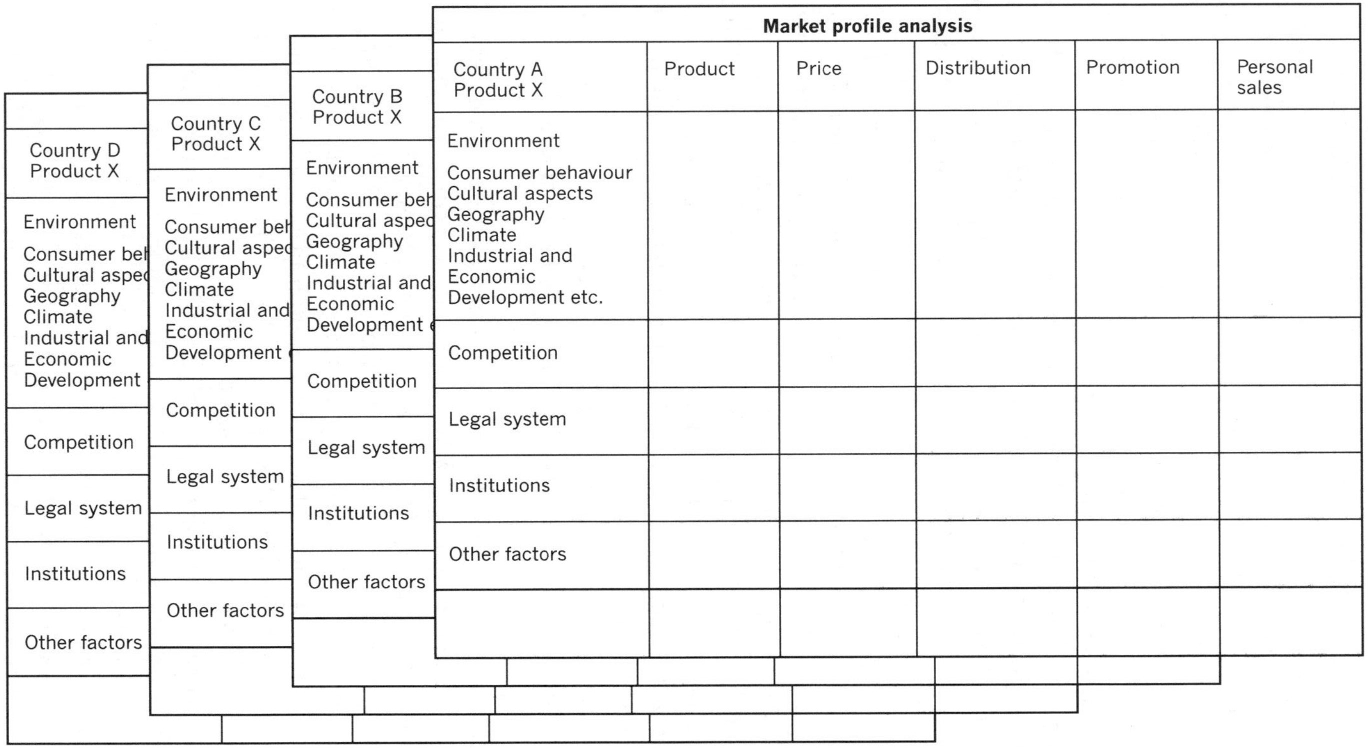
Market profile analysis
Country A
Product X
Product
Price
Distribution
Promotion
Personal
sales
Environment
Consumer behaviour
Cultural aspects
Geography
Climate
Industrial and
Economic
Development etc.
Competition
Legal system
Institutions
Other factors
Country B
Product X
Environment
Consumer beh
Cultural aspec
Geography
Climate
Industrial and
Economic
Development
Competition
Legal system
Institutions
Other factors
Country C
Product X
Environment
Consumer beh
Cultural aspec
Geography
Climate
Industrial and
Economic
Development
Competition
Legal system
Institutions
Other factors
Country D
Product X
Environment
Consumer beh
Cultural aspec
Geography
Climate
Industrial and
Economic
Development
Competition
Legal system
Institutions
Other factors

and must be considered in conjunction with all other factors. Thus all elements are included in the matrix analysis although we are predominantly concerned with the product strategy. For example, a product in one market may be very popular because of its televised promotions but fail in another market because television is unavailable, either for economic reasons or because of a legal ban on television advertising. Similarly with distribution and retailing as mentioned above, not to mention pricing and selling practices.

Prior to launch into a foreign market the product should be considered in the light of the variables affecting its progress, and the matrix analysis provides a clear, though by no means exhaustive overview of these factors. There should therefore be discussion and consideration against every cell of the matrix and due weight given to how these characteristics are likely to affect acceptance. This technique should also pinpoint any need for modification of the product. For example, the colour of the package or its design may offend consumers in a particular market. As Esso discovered some years ago, when it launched its worldwide campaign using the Esso Tiger, this portrayal of the tiger caused offence in Thailand and other Eastern countries which venerated the image of the tiger as sacred. They were thus forced to alter the promotion in those countries.

Thus all aspects of the environment affect each of the elements of the marketing mix in some way and may have to be modified or deleted if necessary.

With regard to the environment, this includes such fundamental characteristics as climate and geography. Cultural aspects and local customs are all-important, as discussed in Chapter 4. All these factors must be scrutinized in turn to ascertain the acceptability of the product.

Economic and industrial development will naturally affect purchase, depending upon the state of sophistication of consumers. The political climate may also prove to be a great obstacle. The Helms–Burton law, for example, which has been proposed to the US Congress, wants to penalize companies doing business with Cuba. Such a law will also affect foreign companies that deal with both countries and is a source of no little controversy.

The competition, both local and imported, is also an important factor. In some developing countries, companies such as United Africa are the main distribution outlets through their trading posts. They also act as agents and distributors for certain goods and competitive items may find it hard to get a foothold in the country.

The legal system will affect such factors as technical standards, commercial radio or television, shopping hours, contracts of employment and, as mentioned above when referring to the proposed Helms–Burton law in the USA, also dictate whether trading is allowed at all. Therefore it is a most important factor and the drafting of any contract should state which legal system governs the contract. Chapter 11 discusses this matter in greater detail.

Another aspect is the existence of marketing institutions, such as advertising agencies or complex distribution systems, department stores, covered markets, out of town hypermarkets and corner shops. Advertising standards institutions and market research agencies all may have an effect on the entry and support of a product from abroad.

Thus careful scrutiny of all these variables is a necessity in international market planning. The market profile analysis, mentioned above, is a useful tool for directing the mind but other sources of information, such as news bulletins or DTI reports, US Department of Commerce Current Export Bulletins, OECD reports, etc. are also to be taken into account. This is why the bottom item is labelled 'Other' in order to allow for any other factors which may prove relevant.

By examining every cell in the matrix, areas of concern which might otherwise be overlooked are highlighted and can be dealt with.

Chapter review

International product strategy has got to consider numerous factors, not only the ones which affect the domestic market, such as consumers' expectations and the competition, but other conditions, such as culture and local attitudes.

One technique for identifying potential problems is the use of the Majaro Matrix which highlights the various factors likely to be encountered in the marketing of a product.

Case study on product policy

Sony's amazing product creativity

Since 1946 the Japanese electronics group Sony, under the leadership of their founder and chairman Akio Morita, has led the world in electronic gadgets. They have repeatedly been able to forecast their consumers' preferences, even before customers became aware of their need for such a product.

The list of brilliant ideas which became translated into marketable products appears endless. Colour television, tape recorders, portable stereos, video cassette recorders, home computers, compact disc players and camcorders have rolled out of their laboratories and factories to satisfy millions of consumers, most of whom had never considered the need for such products before they were made aware of their desirable attributes.

The Sony Walkman, for instance, satisfied the needs of many diverse users, from lonely joggers to bored commuters. None of those had anticipated such a product as necessary until presented with the facility of enjoying music from a pocket-sized device that could be carried about on the person rather than some static item of furniture, as was the case before the Walkman's introduction.

The company is now aiming to repeat this runaway success but cannot determine where the next breakthrough of consumer satisfaction is likely to come from. There are a number of areas in which it has invested considerable resources. For example, there is their Mini Disc, which is a compact disc player the size of a human hand, and the Digital Audio Tape (DAT), a superior quality sound recording tape.

The latter product, however, has not caught on partly because of its high initial cost and partly because of reluctance to accept it by the retail trade, who fear that it may result in new waves of pirated copies owing to the superior sound it produces. Equally, the Mini Disc has run into competitive opposition against Philips who have simultaneously brought out a similar product.

In the field of television, Sony has presented its High Definition Television (HDTV) system which gives a sharper image but there is some doubt that the public really wish to pay the relatively high prices for the benefits of higher quality viewing.

Questions on Sony Case Study

1 Identify and comment on the international marketing principles demonstrated in this case.
2 From the information given in this case study, how do you think Sony develops its product and market strategies?
3 Suggest suitable market segments which Sony might consider for those products which are not immediately successful.

Questions

Section A: Class discussion

1 Briefly describe the attitude of a product-orientated company.
2 What are the characteristics of a sales-orientated company?
3 What are the advantages of Levitt's total product concept theory from the point of view of strategic implementation?
4 Could a core product on its own be successful? If so, under what conditions?
5 Do any of the concepts of product marketing apply equally well to the marketing of services?

Section B: Examination revision

1 What essential factors must the international marketer bear in mind when considering product strategy?
2 What two axes form the structure of the Majaro model? Explain how they interact to assist in decision making.
3 Is total globalization of products a possibility? What are the factors that may oppose this objective?
4 Why is it so important for marketers to aim for brand image?
5 In a market or country of your choice, compare the different cells of the Majaro Matrix and discuss your findings. Compare these with two similar cells in another market.

References

Dibb, S., Symkin, L., Pride, W.M. and Ferrell, O.C. (1994) *Marketing – European edition*, Boston and London: Houghton Mifflin Co.

Douglas, S. and Craig, C.S. (1995) *Global Marketing Strategies*, McGraw-Hill, Chapter 10.

Majaro, S. (1993) International Marketing. A Stategic Approach to World Markets Revised Edition, Routledge.

International promotion strategies

9

❑ CHAPTER PREVIEW

Promotion is an essential part of the marketing mix and form the aspect of communication with the market, which is so essential to achieving consumer satisfaction. Communication with any target group varies enormously for a variety of reasons, linguistic, cultural, legal and so forth. These are discussed in some detail. In conclusion, because of its particular importance to international marketing, the specific advantages and organization of exhibitions and trade fairs are also reviewed.

This chapter relates to topics discussed in other chapters such as communication with the market, cultural impact on marketing operations, product strategy and the marketing of services.

❑ BY THE END OF THIS CHAPTER YOU SHOULD:

■ Appreciate the importance of promotion to the marketing mix

■ Consider the particular target audiences that exist worldwide

■   **Be aware of the pitfalls of blanket promotional strategies**

■   **Note the differentials of promotional factors and facilities in different countries**

■   **Give due consideration to the importance of exhibitions and trade fairs to the international marketer.**   ❏

Introduction

Communication with the appropriate segment of the market to obtain consumer satisfaction is a cornerstone of the marketing concept. This is just as true of marketing in foreign countries as it is for the domestic market. However, the international marketer must beware of the self-reference criterion and consider specifically the target groups in the country, or countries, concerned. In fact, some countries, such as Switzerland with its four official languages and Belgium with two, French and Flemish, provide a good example of how the segment may differ even within the one country.

The socio-economic groups prevailing in Europe and the United States vary greatly in proportion and structure from other parts of the world. In some countries for instance there is a small elite within a large population, or else there are a few urban centres where there is a demand for some advanced products such as cars or refrigerators as against the remainder of the country which could be rural and mainly agricultural.

On top of that, there are many other cultural, legal and linguistic factors which must be taken into consideration as well as the particular use of the product in that market. For example, bicycles which are used for leisure purposes in the industrialized West are used as working vehicles in less developed countries. Another example of product differentiation by usage is in the UK where beer is an alcoholic drink subject to legal restrictions whereas it is considered as a cool drink in Spain, comparative and competitive with soft drinks like orangeade and Coca-Cola.

This complex structure of intertwining cultural and societal conditions means that any promotional or advertising campaign has to be considered in the light of all these factors and not blindly replicated from current or recent operations in other countries.

The communication process

A basic model of communication, as shown in Figure 9.1, will identify the elements in the process and make it possible to modify to adapt to particular situations.

Any marketing and promotional campaign which is aimed at another market must give due consideration to each of these elements.

Source and target market

For instance, the source of the message to be aimed at the target market will be the marketers and their proposed intentions, or objectives, whether these are for market entry or consolidation or even expansion of market share. Whatever the objectives, the campaign will have to be tailored for the particular requirements of the operation.

The target market is the group of potential consumers and their variants in accordance with their geographical situation, their segment of the market, their language, culture, legal system, social structure and other factors as mentioned above.

Figure 9.1 Elements in the international promotion process

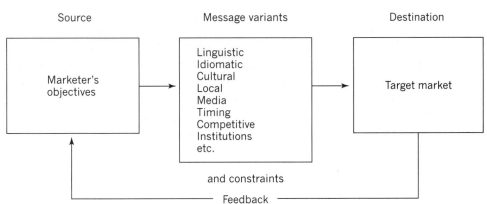

Message variants

The operation has got to allow for a number of variants or differentials, some of which will be briefly discussed below but, in effect, require serious and considered thought and application.

Linguistic differentials

Even between the USA and the UK there are differences in expressions. For instance, the boot of a car in the UK is called the trunk in the USA, and what British people call a lift Americans call an elevator. The expression 'Goes like a bomb' has directly opposite meanings in the UK and USA. In the UK this means that it is a very lively item whereas in the USA it means that it is a non-starter. The list is endless, so that any company in the USA and the UK contemplating campaigns in both countries must take these differences into account and not assume that direct translation is automatically understood.

The differences with translation into other languages compounds the difficulties. Some terms are not directly translatable and in some cases lead to hilarious results. 'Come alive with Pepsi' is said to have been translated as 'Leap out of the grave' in some Asian languages. The use of certain words in the product name may cause offence in other languages. Rolls-Royce could not market its Silver Mist model in Germany as 'mist' means excrement in German.

Suffice to say that the above are extreme examples and all advertising copy should be professionally translated before the launch of a campaign.

Other problems may occur when transferring advertising messages into non-European languages. Arabic, for instance, reads from right to left. Any artwork depicting a sequence of events, such as in a Mars bar advertisement in the Arab media. Arabs would read this particular advertisement as a busy man obtaining energy to play football after working hours by eating a glucose-rich Mars bar. To the European this would appear nonsensical, with someone playing football, partaking of a Mars bar and ending tired at his desk as a result.

Cultural differentials

These variants reflect the use of such items as the exposed female form in advertisements or even symbols which are revered in a particular society and should not be used for trivial connections. Elephants in India are considered holy by some people and their appearance in advertisements would be bound to cause offence, as would lightly dressed ladies advertising beauty products in strict traditional societies. There again the marketer has to be guided by a representative or agent to advise as to the acceptable form of artwork for the market concerned.

Legal differentials

Some of these variants are invariably connected with cultural factors. The design of advertisements in some traditional and conservative societies may restrict the use of scantily clad females. A greater involvement by the law is the restriction on the advertising of tobacco and alcoholic products. The law may also govern the pricing of products and also the claims made by the product about its effectiveness.

As with language and culture, the legal position as to what constitutes an acceptable advertisement has to be cleared with experts within the country where the advertisement will be shown.

Media variants

It must not be supposed that the media in each country is identical. The number of newspapers and magazines may vary from country to country. Commercial television may not be available in every market and in other cases the time available for commercial breaks may be restricted.

For industrial products the range of specialist magazines may be very limited and therefore advertising in the local newspaper will obviously reduce its effectiveness. Other forms of promotion, such as exhibitions, are preferable in these cases and will be discussed in greater detail below.

Where literacy is low, newspaper readership will not be so extensive. Posters, however, are predominantly popular in the Middle East where the weather is conducive to an outdoor lifestyle. Radio is also a popular medium in that part of the world as the culture there accepts radios which blare out at every street corner to passers-by.

Other media variants could be the availability of sophisticated printing and colour processing or paper quality in local magazines and posters.

Timing

Some markets which are geographically located at long distances from the exporting country will have to time their promotions to coincide with the delivery of the products. It is useless to advertise a product which will not be immediately available in the shops. The lead times for the placing of advertising space and time on radio and television must also be taken into consideration when planning a campaign for goods which are due to arrive at a certain date.

Timing on a broader level is reflected in comparisons of the different stages of the product life cycle between markets. Products in the maturity stage in one market, with their appropriate marketing strategies, may be at the introductory or growth stages in other markets and will therefore require quite different advertising messages.

Other

There are numerous other factors to be considered and again, they will require research and consultation with people on the spot before final decisions are taken. Marketing institutions like advertising or market research agencies as well as the distribution system need to be available. Does the market have department stores and supermarkets or does it rely on corner shops and bazaars? Alternatively, it could be a mixture, which again could affect the promotion.

The competition, whether local or from other importers, is a further consideration, as is the economic climate. Hence the number of factors may vary considerably and cannot be assumed to exactly reflect the home market.

Exhibitions and trade fairs

A most effective method of promoting one's product is by exhibiting it at an international trade fair. Here potential customers can see the products for themselves, feel them and see them actually demonstrated.

Furthermore, in many cases, some of the above questions regarding the complexities of the market can be answered when exhibiting at a trade fair. The company and its executives, by taking part in the exhibition, can immerse themselves in the local environment and conditions, meeting and discussing matters of mutual interest with local businessmen and customers.

Such is the importance of international exhibitions that most industrial countries provide assistance to their exporters to help them exhibit their products to foreign buyers. In fact, the planned economies of the old Soviet Bloc would use trade fairs in their countries as part of their overall plan, even to the extent of specifying what products they wished to see exhibited and directing their officials to inspect them.

The next part of this chapter is accordingly devoted to this subject.

The strategic dimension of international exhibitions

Many textbooks on international marketing make only passing reference to the significance of international exhibitions for an organization which is seeking to improve its performance in international marketing. However, in most industries, firms with a record of success devote vast resources to trade fairs and frequently receive a high percentage of their annual orders through them, either directly – orders taken on the stand – or indirectly through orders which are sent in later as a result of a buyer's visit to the stand.

It is true that some executives who are deeply involved with the organization of trade fairs do not always grasp the strategical significance of these for their company. But this may have more to do with the operational nature of their specific function in relation to trade fairs than the fact that the organization itself does not understand this relation.

The theory of international trade fairs may be divided into five sections:

1 Should the organization be using a stand at an exhibition? This will largely depend on anticipated cost-effectiveness.
2 If yes, then which exhibition is the right one? This will depend on a number of factors, including where the firm wants to be in five years' time and which industry it will be in then. In some industries, changes are continuously taking place.
3 Pre-fair preparations, stand design.

4   Essential activities during the fair.
5   The follow-up; evaluation.

Should the organization be using a stand? Does exhibiting give us an advantage?

The most important question is whether the cost of hiring a stand is worth it or not. This is not easy to decide for companies who have not done so before, as there are many unknown factors. The following are some considerations which will help us come to a decision:

● Do our main competitors in the industry use an exhibition effectively and profitably?
● Have we a specific aim in view which we wish to realize using an exhibition?
● Do we intend to make this exhibition a one-off, or are we going to work out a strategy for exhibitions?
● Is there any cheaper alternative which might prove more effective, e.g. our own exhibition in a hotel?

If we are a company which has soared into the ascendancy and already enjoy a well-known reputation, then our own private show may be the answer. Otherwise, for many firms, the most crucial question is, do the leading firms in our industry use an exhibition?

Which is the right exhibition for us?

Here substantial market research, both primary and secondary, is necessary. In addition to the knowledge we already have concerning the potential impact of an exhibition on the market where it is held and the neighbouring target markets, we need to consult with our agents, distributors or wholly owned subsidiaries, to try to ascertain the potential benefits of exhibiting. We must also beware if the benefits they are all seeking are very different because this will lead to differences in the design of the stand. The research carried out with the organization running the fairs is among the most important. These days, serious exhibition organizers have comprehensive databases concerning visitors to their past exhibitions. This information can help us decide which is the right exhibition for us. Information which we would ideally like to obtain about their previous visitors includes:

- Firm represented
- Size and type of business it is in
- Function of visitor in firm
- If not buyer, what is his influence in buying decision?
- What range of products is he interested in?
- Does his firm take buying decisions at exhibitions or at some other time?

While it is important to know which firms have exhibited at this exhibition in the past, details of the visitors are more important and these can be obtained, for a fee, direct from the organizers. Since the cost of exhibitions is high we should consider the possibility of joining a group of exhibitors, whether from our industry or organized by various national governments, such as the Fairs and Promotions Branch of the DTI, so as to reduce costs. Once the decision as to which exhibition has been taken, then no time must be lost in starting to design the stand and book hotel accommodation locally for stand staff. The former is an area where the advice of consultants is invaluable and certainly worth the price the first time round. While it may be nice to have a stand that stands out from the crowd, we do not wish to have one that does so for the wrong reasons.

Planning and preparation for the exhibition

However, before we can give our consultants their brief we need to prioritize the aims of our stand. These could be:

- Sales on the stand in figures or units
- Sales within three months from enquiries there
- Awareness of our organization
- A specific range of our products
- Our new products
- Finding an agent
- Acquiring information about the market
- A combination of the above.

Since stands are expensive we must also decide which are the vital areas for us among:

- Display area
- Demonstration areas
- Entertainment areas
- Quiet private areas for negotiations
- Space for potential customers to circulate

As well as stand design and preparation the following areas are vital for planning:

- Training of sales staff specifically for the stand
- Availability of sales staff speaking the appropriate languages
- Preparation of sales literature in the appropriate languages and quantity in good time
- Invitations to potential customers in good time
- Booking of hotel accommodation near to the exhibition

All the above should be discussed with our agents and distributors well in advance.

During the fair

We scarcely need to say that the effectiveness and success of the activities during the exhibition is vital.

Let us examine some of these activities. The activity of the staff on the stand needs to be carefully coordinated. The hours of an exhibition tend to be long and in addition a great deal of entertainment may be needed in the evening. But the last thing a company needs is tired-looking executives on the stand, so a rota for who does what is essential. It is during the fair itself that the training of personnel shows its value. A stand is a very different environment from the usual one for most salespeople. Usually salespeople meet buyers on the buyers' territory. An exhibition is more like common ground.

One of the most important aspects of the exhibition is eliciting the correct information from all visitors. To ensure that this happens in fact the sales staff will be trained and provided, if appropriate, with forms which will remind them of which information is vital and which is desirable. If a visitor to the stand is an important one with an appointment, then no time should be lost in introducing the visitor to the person with whom he or she has the appointment. All details of enquiries must be accurately recorded, which is not always easy in the bustle of a trade fair, especially as stand visitors seem to arrive in clusters rather than at regular intervals.

After the fair

Much of the effectiveness of post-fair activity depends on how accurately information has been recorded during the fair, and whether the right information has been recorded.

The following areas need to be examined as soon as possible after the fair:

- Order enquiries
- Enquiries about products which potential customers would like to order but which we do not manufacture now
- Complaints
- Enquiries from potential agents/distributors

However, the most important overall factor is assessing the overall cost-effectiveness of the exhibition. This can only be done effectively if we have clearly spelled out beforehand in writing the specific quantifiable aims of the fair in terms of sales targets, among other things. Stand design, staff training and literature will all come under scrutiny while the staff who were on the stand can still remember how effective they seemed to be.

Stands at exhibitions are always expensive in terms of hire charges and the enormous amount of staff and expertise needed there. The cost must therefore be justifiable. But if it is, then having a stand at an international exhibition can be a most effective marketing tool in international marketing.

Personal selling

At international trade fairs as well as at other times the company relies upon the knowledge of the market gained by the sales executive who covers that territory. International salespeople, even more than their domestic counterparts, are ambassadors not only for their firm but also for their country.

As such, they must have cultural awareness and sensitivity. Ideally they should have some linguistic expertise even if it is rudimentary. An attempt to communicate in the host country's language, even a few sentences, always pleases and paves the way for pleasant discussion and negotiations.

As well as possessing these required social skills, the international sales executive must be fully knowledgeable on his or her product. Without the possibility of instant and direct communication with the company, there are occasions when technical matters must be explained and important decisions taken on the spot. Most personal selling in an international situation is of a business-to-business nature or, as it is sometimes termed, organizational marketing. Therefore, the ability to negotiate on behalf of the company is an important attribute.

Chapter review

Promotion is a fundamental aspect of the marketing mix and the various promotional strategies are the means of communicating with the market. In international marketing, however, there are many variables, of a cultural as well as a commercial nature, which preclude the automatic transference of the promotional message from one market to another.

Due care and consideration must therefore be given to ensure that the promotional message is clearly understood.

A specific and effective form of communication in international marketing is exhibiting at international trade fairs and exhibitions.

Personal selling is also very important, with salespeople having to have the necessary attributes of cultural awareness, product knowledge and negotiating skills as well as linguistic ability.

Questions

Section A: Class discussion

1 Summarize the main elements of an international marketing promotion strategy.

2 What differences exist between the promotional strategy of an indirect export policy and a direct export policy?
3 Examine the main principles of personal selling in international marketing.
4 Briefly describe the three main stages of the stand activity of an exhibitor at an international exhibition.
5 Do sales staff need special training for international exhibitions?

Section B: Examination revision

1 Comment on the statement that international exhibitions are the driving force of a successful firm's international promotional policy.
2 What essential differences exist in personal selling between international marketing and domestic marketing?
3 'International marketing advertising must be global to be effective.' Discuss.
4 'Decisions about international exhibitions are strategic rather than tactical in their impact.' Examine this statement, with examples.
5 What aspect of international promotions is often most important for SMEs?

Illustrative Case Study

Eli Lilly, the US manufacturers of the anti-depressant drug Prozak, have started to promote it to the general public by means of a double-page spread in certain magazines. These advertisements depict a dark and rainy scene on one side with the slogan 'Depression hurts' and on the other page a bright sunny sky with the message 'Prozak can help'.

Their advertising objective is to create greater awareness of the product's benefits to the general public and such promotion aimed at the community at large is generally allowed in the USA, although the product itself is only available through a doctor's prescription.

In the United Kingdom and other European countries, however, only drugs which are available over the counter (OTC) are allowed by law to be advertised direct to the consumer. The reasons for allowing these drugs to be both advertised and sold over the counter by chemists without prescription is that they have been proven over time not to be harmful unless abused by the user.

Illustrative Case Study continued

The only way that prescription drugs can be promoted is in specialist medical journals or communicated through events attended by the medical profession. Doctors in European countries maintain that it is dangerous to allow the lay public such information as they will demand such drugs from their general practitioners (GPs) without complete knowledge of the drug's properties or even whether they are appropriate for the complaint. American culture tends to embrace a degree of scepticism which aggressively questions diagnoses, thereby leading to greater demand for the drug. However, doctors maintain that these drugs do not necessarily help everyone and can even have harmful side effects.

The American drugs industry counters such arguments with certain facts. They maintain that OTC drugs have been increasingly advertised for many years without any serious danger to the public being recorded. Furthermore, they justify their communication to the lay public because many doctors do not necessarily keep abreast of developments in the medical field and therefore patients' demand for new drugs can prove beneficial.

The debate is complicated by the fact that in Britain and other European countries, unlike the United States, there are national health schemes in force. Governments would therefore be reluctant to allow promotions which would tend to increase health expenditure. Again, drug companies counter these fears by maintaining that higher use of drugs will lower costs of surgery.

(This case was adapted from an article in *The Economist* 9 of August 1997.)

Questions

1   To what other countries might Eli Lilly try to adapt its current promotion? What particular factors may be appropriate?
2   Who would be wary of such types of promotions and what might be the direct results of these?
3   What other types of promotion might manufacturers of prescription drugs use to communicate with their markets?

References

Onkvisit, S. and Shaw, J.J. (1989) *International Marketing*, Merrill Publishing Co., Chapter 14.

10

Pricing strategies in international marketing

❑ CHAPTER PREVIEW

This chapter considers the variables which are additional to the basic pricing strategies such as penetration, skimming and what the market will bear. The use of intermediaries and their possibly conflicting objectives are reviewed, as are the additional costs which must be borne for the setting of a price to the consumer in a foreign market.

Other methods such as the use of marginal costing to set a penetration price and transfer prices for the overall strategy of a multinational corporation's objectives are explained, as are their pitfalls. Finally, a brief indication of the tender bidding process is shown, together with the differing objectives of buyer and seller in such situations.

This chapter relates to product strategy and technical aspects of international marketing.

❑ BY THE END OF THIS CHAPTER YOU SHOULD:

■ Appreciate the different conditions leading to an appropriate strategy

- ■ Consider pricing strategies when intermediaries are involved in the distribution process
- ■ Be aware of the extra costs involved when setting prices internationally
- ■ Consider the benefits and implications of marginal pricing for market penetration
- ■ Be informed as to how MNCs can implement transfer pricing strategies for their own objectives
- ■ Understand the procedures and objectives involved in tender bid pricing for international projects.   ❏

Pricing as an integral marketing strategy

International marketing, being an extension of basic marketing principles, gives due regard to those established principles, of which pricing strategies are a cornerstone. Briefly, such strategies vary with the situation and objectives of the company. Many organizations use cost-plus calculations to arrive at a suitable price although this is a somewhat short-sighted method and potentially hazardous for the launching of new products. There are various other strategies that could be pursued which could render higher returns or achieve particular objectives. For instance, when a new and exclusive product is introduced and the competition is weak, it is possible for the marketer to reap extra profits by adopting a skimming, or creaming of profits strategy by inflating the price.

Alternatively, when there is a strong competitor or the need to fight off competition, profits will be minimized, or even forgone by using a penetration or predatory price. Eventually the broad view is to set the price at what the market will bear. The above briefly described strategies apply everywhere and marketers study their consumers before deciding upon an appropriate strategy. However, all these considerations are compounded and complicated by the conditions prevailing in foreign markets and other variables affecting international trade.

Markets may be sophisticated or primitive. They may vary enormously even within one country. Local preferences vary, as will the number of competitors. Legal and environmental factors will come to bear, as will be discussed in Chapter 11. For many SMEs the penetration and handling of the market may be in the hands of an intermediary such as an agent or distributor.

Pricing when marketing through an agent

When the marketing in a country is handled by an exclusive agent, the principal should be well advised to rely upon the agent's local knowledge and appreciation. It was, after all, the reason for the agent's appointment in the first place. The agent's role would be to advise on a price which suits the market, whether skimming, penetrating or following the competition.

Having said that, due regard must be given to the fact that the principal's and the agent's objectives may differ. The principal doubtless wishes to reap the maximum benefit from sales of its product to the market, while the agent may wish for a higher turnover in order to obtain the maximum commission. Because the agent does not have title to the goods, he or she will have to accept the price imposed by the principal, but this would certainly result in loss of motivation and efficiency.

Furthermore, the agent is expected to understand the market, for instance where cultural factors require that prices are not immediately accepted by consumers but haggled over before a sale. In such cases the prices will be inflated to allow for eventual reduction.

Such variations can only be handled by constant monitoring of the market and its conditions, by the principal. In the long run, however, it is the harmonious relationship between these two parties which will yield the best results. The need for good communication against a background of distance, cultural, legal and environmental difference is paramount in such cases.

Marketing through a distributor

An additional problem, similar yet more complex than the above, arises when dealing with distributors. As mentioned previously, when discussing the functions of distributors, the goods available on the market are the purchased property of the distributors and accordingly they have the perfect right to set the price that suits them. Here again, the problems mentioned above also arise, in that the objectives of the distributor and those of the principal may differ. The distributor in this case may wish for the highest return on his/her purchase, while the principal may wish for a lower market price in order to obtain quicker turnaround for its products. The principal in this case is powerless to impose the price it wants and can only attempt to persuade, while being aware at the same time that the distributor is a local inhabitant of the market and should have a better knowledge of the current situation.

There is no cut and dried solution to such situations. They differ so much according to circumstances. Again, the requirement for good relations which will result in friendly and positive negotiations is paramount. Each party would present their case and a compromise must be reached. Failure to do so will lead to mistrust and lack of effort. Unlike multinational corporations which have their own subsidiary companies staffed by their own employees and can therefore impose their desired conditions, SMEs have to work with intermediaries and rely on their goodwill and cooperation to maximize market potential. Therefore the need to set prices agreeable to both parties, taking due consideration of the conditions prevailing in the market, as with all other aspects of the marketing mix when dealing with parties outside the company's authority, is a crucial factor in international marketing.

Composition of price

Given the broad situations mentioned above, when prices have to be set with regard to the working conditions and all other factors influencing the price decision, there are nevertheless certain conditions which must be taken into consideration when dealing with foreign markets. It is an obvious fact that goods going to a destination other than the domestic market will have to bear the cost of transportation which, in most cases, is greater than that of the goods transported to domestic users. Therefore, we give a brief outline of some essential costs and some basic make-up of prices for goods destined abroad.

The following list of essential costs and considerations applies in most cases, with variations according to negotiated agreements or conditions, and it is imperative that such basic costs and factors are borne in mind when setting or negotiating a price for a particular market. Comments regarding reasons and possible variations are discussed for each item in the list.

Although each item is essential to the composition and setting of the final price to the consumer, there are occasions, such as predatory or penetration strategies, or where marginal pricing is undertaken as a strategy (see below), where some of these items are either modified or waived.

Nevertheless, the following list serves as a suitable model for consideration of each item and its worth in a negotiated situation.

- **Ex works price** This is the direct costs of manufacture plus any costs of modification of the product for a particular market, e.g. heavy-duty batteries for vehicles destined for very cold climates or fitting of extra fine filters on engines going to desert locations.
- **Appropriate allocation of company's overheads** This could be a requirement for a cost or profit centre of the organization. Such a division or department may have to make a contribution to the overall organization, e.g. the export department may have to set aside a percentage of its revenue towards the costs of running the department.

    Possibly each department may be required to contribute towards R&D costs.

    However, some of those costs may not apply to the export department, such as contributions to promotions or showrooms, which are only relevant to domestic sales (or sales to other markets).

    Therefore there should be both an addition to as well as a possible deduction from certain departmental costs.
- **Special market costs** Possibly instituted for emphasis on the potential and importance that the firm places on the market, e.g. advertising and other promotions targeted to the market. In some cases additional costs are imposed for anticipated servicing problems owing to harsh environmental conditions or poor maintenance facilities.
- **Agency commission** This item is confidential and should never be divulged to anyone outside the organization. Customers would demand a discount on the basis that they approached the company directly without the assistance of the agent. Agreement to this would compromise the principal and sour relations between them and the agent if the

agent ever found out (which he or she most certainly would).

Equally, a commission should be reserved even when no agent exists. This is because at some time an agent may be appointed and customers would rightly demand a price similar to a prior sale which had no commission included. The company would then have to compensate the agent and thereby lose a profit on those sales.

- **Appropriate profit margin on sales**   As discussed above, this is a matter for negotiation between principal and agent and depends upon the current situation in the market. This will dictate the amount of sales turnover, which directly affects the agent's remuneration. This is a delicate matter and must be handled very diplomatically as failure to do so will result in the agent's demotivation. However, it is also a matter for constant review and the amount of sales generated by a wise decision will benefit all parties.

  The above will not affect distributors who will doubtless purchase at the cost mentioned against 'special market costs' above and arrange for their own packing and shipment of the goods, which they will then sell in their own market. However, even in this case, there should be a discussion between principal and distributor with regard to an appropriate margin.

  Even though the principal has no authority to set prices, in this instance the overriding consideration of a successful marketing operation should be the basis for a mutual agreement on the margin and the final price to the consumer.

- **Special export packaging costs**   Goods going by sea or having to be handled at various stages of their journey must be encased in protective packing to avoid damage or deterioration.

The terms mentioned below are INCOTERMS (International Chamber of Terms of Sale).

- **FOB or FCA charges**   All costs incurred in the handling and transportation of the goods from the factory to a specified port of shipment (FOB or Free on Board) and on to the ship. Otherwise, all costs incurred in the transportation and handling of the goods from the factory gates to an inland container depot (FCA or Free to Carrier) or to a specified airport.
- **CIF or CIP charges**   These costs include the FOB or FCA charges and are additional charges for transporting the goods by sea (CIF or

Cost Insurance and Freight) to a foreign port.

Alternatively, CIP charges (or Carriage and Insurance Paid) refer to container loads which are transported in a variety of ways (multi-modal transport). From the factory the goods are sent to a container depot where they are put into containers and are then transported by road, rail or sea to a specified destination.

- **DDP charges** (Delivered Duty Paid) These are the most inclusive charges which incorporate FOB or FCA charges and CIF or CIP charges as well as local landing and handling charges, customs duties and all costs, right to the importer's premises. (This was formerly known as Franco Domicile.)
- **Wholesale or retail mark-ups where applicable**

Whether using an agent, distributor or own subsidiary company these charges are a permanent consideration. Costs may possibly be reduced by bulk shipments or special agreements with the carriers or shipping companies but ultimately they will have to figure in the price.

Figure 10.1 shows a typical example of a top-up model of price calculation for overseas markets.

Marginal costing technique for penetrating markets

Given the variety of costs mentioned above, exporters trying to penetrate difficult markets may be tempted to offer reduced prices for their product by adopting a method of marginal costing. This is to select a batch of goods destined for a specific market and ignore the fixed costs, only considering the variable costs, in order to offer lower prices.

Such a decision will definitely reduce the price of a product considerably, as demonstrated by the diagrams in Figure 10.2.

Instead of a product having to bear both fixed and variable costs as is the normal procedure, the goods destined for a certain market will be exempt from the fixed costs, allowing these to be spread to the goods for the domestic market. The resulting lower price will serve to penetrate a difficult market or serve some other promotional strategy.

Figure 10.1 Typical example of the top-up model of price calculation for overseas markets based on £100 ex-works. Figures and items vary according to condition. Also, price reductions can be effected by economies of scale if the products prove popular.

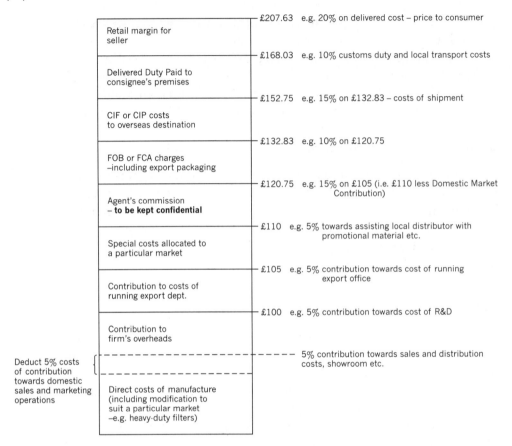

Pitfalls to be avoided

While this method undoubtedly provides a lower priced product it cannot be denied that the domestic market will bear these costs and the corporate accountant will have to be persuaded that such a decision is in order. Moreover, it may leave the company liable to complaints of dumping by local governments or even by the World Trade Organization.

Also, there are real risks involved. Sales would rise to the point that the batches destined for the market would increase to the point of taking

Figure 10.2 Penetration pricing by means of marginal pricing

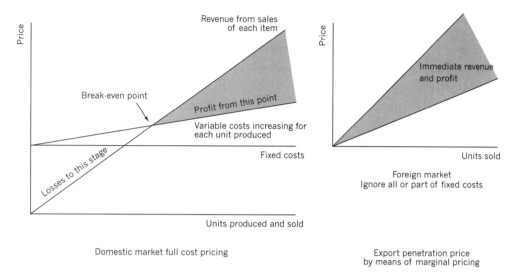

Domestic market full cost pricing

Export penetration price
by means of marginal pricing

up most or all of the firm's production output. In such a case the company may find itself producing and selling at a total loss for each item going to the foreign market. It has also been known for such reduced items to attract buyers from adjacent countries or even from the exporter's own country, thus rendering such a venture without profit.

Therefore such a pricing strategy, while having some merit in exceptional cases, must be adopted with great caution and careful monitoring.

Transfer pricing

Unlike the above technique which applies mainly to struggling SMEs, the use of transfer pricing is a potentially profit-enhancing method for MNCs. Where a multinational operates in many countries through its own subsidiary companies, it can sell them such products as machinery or raw materials, or even services such as financial support, etc. and charge accordingly through an internal account.

Thus a subsidiary can show a greater or lesser profit, or obtain goods from abroad (the head office or other subsidiaries) at higher or lower prices. The prices will be set by the head office and may bear no relation to the real value of the goods, the main aim being to increase or decrease a subsidiary's profit. This will enable the subsidiary to pay a lower tax on its profits, or it can be used as a method of repatriation of funds.

Alternatively it could enable a subsidiary to import goods at a lower price and pay lower customs duties.

Transfer pricing is illustrated in Figure 10.3.

Naturally, host governments frown upon such procedures and check closely upon all such operations. Most multinationals avoid such blatant

Figure 10.3 Transfer pricing by MNIs. Diagram indicates known funds can be transferred between subsidiary companies by means of differing prices to further the organization objectives.

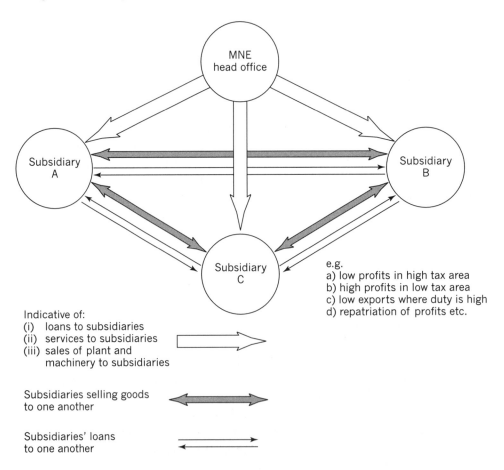

MNE
head office

Subsidiary
A

Subsidiary
B

Subsidiary
C

e.g.
a) low profits in high tax area
b) high profits in low tax area
c) low exports where duty is high
d) repatriation of profits etc.

Indicative of:
(i)   loans to subsidiaries
(ii) services to subsidiaries
(iii) sales of plant and
      machinery to subsidiaries

Subsidiaries selling goods
to one another

Subsidiaries' loans
to one another

deception and robbery of the host country's revenue. However, it is mentioned here as one possible, though unethical, pricing strategy.

Tender bid pricing

This is a procedure occurring when a government or large organization wishes to purchase goods at the lowest possible price and avoid suppliers colluding to push the price up, as well as having its officials favouring a particular supplier.

The general method, with some variations, is for the government to put out a tender, that is, to announce that they are in need of some product and provide specifications. Generally the government states that it is a sealed bid, which means that the suppliers or companies bidding for the contract submit their price under a sealed envelope. This ensures that no one knows or can influence the price of the individual offer.

At a certain time on a certain day, the bids are opened in the presence of a high official and the most suitable offer selected to be given the contract.

Making up a price in such instances may prompt companies to make offers at a loss or at break even or very little profit because of such behavioural factors as prestige or the potential for further contracts. Alternatively, companies having production problems may desire not being selected at this particular instance but not wish to be left out of future invitations to tender. In such cases they may submit an offer at an unacceptably high price.

Currency fluctuation

The currency factor also affects pricing of products in a foreign market. Current strength or weakness of the local currency will affect the market price and although the subject is one of great complexity the matter is, again, one for discussion between exporters and their intermediaries or a multinational's head office and its local management.

Conclusion

Pricing of products depends upon market conditions and in international marketing pricing strategies are compounded by a number of factors such as intermediaries, transportation costs, and cultural and legal constraints. The marketer must therefore study the situation, often with the assistance of agents, distributors or local managers, in order to set the correct price for the market.

Chapter review

The pricing of products destined for foreign markets depends upon many factors, such as the method of distribution and transportation as well as the relationship between the supplier's head office and the local importing organization. Other methods of adapting pricing strategies according to varying local conditions are discussed.

Questions

Section A: Class discussion

1   Why must principals take into consideration the views of an agent as regards pricing?
2   What makes the setting of prices particularly sensitive when the intermediary is a distributor?
3   Why do governments or large organizations choose to purchase goods through issuing a tender?
4   State the pros and cons of a decision to price by use of marginal costing.
5   Why would transfer pricing affect a host country's economy?

Section B: Examination revision

1   How would the current strength of a currency affect the sales of products? Give examples, real or fictitious, to illustrate your answer.
2   What aspects of a foreign country's culture would be likely to affect pricing policy and what do you think an agent would suggest to his or her principal in such an instance?
3   Given that additional costs are likely to increase prices to a foreign consumer, what options are open to a company wishing to enter a foreign market?

Case study

'Well, it seems to have paid off,' said Jim Parkes to himself. On his desk lay an enquiry from Ishiguru Fuji of Fucha-Shi, Osaka, a small Japanese manufacturer of electrical equipment but a member of the vast Keiretsu or Japanese conglomerate, Mitsubishi.

As Export Manager of the RS Group, a wholesale distributor of electrical products, one of his first decisions on becoming Export Manager was to visit Japan and appoint a commission agent to promote business in that country. Getting a toe-hold in the Japanese market would undoubtedly be a feather in his cap and an important boost for the company.

Although the initial enquiry was for a modest amount it seemed very likely that it was for goods to be incorporated into Fucha-Shi's main electrical equipment, which in turn could be required by other members of the conglomerate.

Fucha-Shi were enquiring about the best price and delivery for a consignment of 10 000 metres of four-core heavy-duty steel wire with flame-retardant insulation.

The ex-works price for a 100-metre reel of this specification cable is £187.00 and delivery from the factory will be 8/10 weeks. Each reel weighs 48.4 kg and has a diameter of 30 cm and length of 60 cm. A 12½% discount is appropriate for an order of this quantity of cable. Insurance costs are set at 1% of the total cost but it is usual to cover for 10% of the total cost because of the time and effort spent in cases of recovery of the claim.

Agency commission is 10% and export packing, administrative costs and other premiums are set at 5% of total cost. The shipping agents advise that shipping rates to Osaka are £18.80 per metric tonne.

Questions

1 From the information given, work out the total cost to the customer.
2 What is the total price in Yen? Work out the spot rates from a current newspaper or obtain information from a bank.
3 In view of the importance of this order for the RS Group, are there any other strategies that could be pursued? Discuss the possibilities.

(This is a totally fictitious case adapted from a previous examination question. All names and details were taken from a technical publication.)

4 Using real or fictitious examples, discuss the various reasons why companies would wish to avoid obtaining a particular contract, yet are eager to submit a bid for a government tender.

5 'Distributors are a law unto themselves.' Discuss the validity of this statement from the point of view of a principal. What suggestions can you offer to the principal?

References

Phillips, C., Doole, I. and Lowe, R. (1994) *International Marketing Strategy*, International Thomson Business Press, Chapter 11.

11

Legal aspects of international marketing

❏ CHAPTER PREVIEW

Legal systems have evolved over time and in every country, each country framing its own laws to provide a stable environment for its citizens' lives and transactions.

In the case of international marketing, which by its very nature involves citizens and organizations of different countries, the legal systems may differ, thereby causing disputes and problems over payment. The avoidance of such problems must be considered at the outset of any marketing operation.

This chapter relates to product, promotional and pricing strategy as discussed elsewhere in this book. In fact every commercial transaction is performed under a legal obligation and in international operations the legal systems governing contracts will vary according to the will of the parties involved.

❏ BY THE END OF THIS CHAPTER YOU SHOULD:

■ Be aware of the importance of a legal contract to a marketing operation

- ■ Understand that laws differ between nations because of history, customs and culture
- ■ Consider the implications of the law that governs the contract
- ■ Appreciate the possibilities of the parties in a dispute to resort to arbitration.   ❏

Introduction

International marketing operations essentially mean agreements between parties of different nations and therefore differing legal systems, each country having evolved its own system through its history, culture, religion, politics and customs.

Every country's law has the aim of preserving the social order and providing a broad model of individual, and corporate, conduct. The law establishes the nature of property and other rights of people and organizations in a society, endeavouring to narrow the range of uncertainty of expectations in cases of disagreement, thereby rendering possible the stability of a society.

International operations demand contracts for delivery of goods, quality and performance of products and services, provision for adequate support, purchase of property and other products and a myriad number of unforeseen circumstances. Disputes seem out of place at times when parties get together for a business venture but none the less they do occur and should be settled with as little loss of time and expense as possible.

Conflict of laws

There are four basic variations of law in the world, with countries adopting a combination in most cases.

- ● Civil or Napoleonic Code Law, as is used in most parts of the world. This legal code has a very ancient basis being originally formulated at the time of the Roman Empire. This was subsequently modified by Napoleon who imposed it upon the countries he conquered at the time and who then adopted its principles. This code relies upon a set of immutable written laws applicable to every occasion.

- The English legal system or Common Law derives from the time of the Norman Conquest and was never altered because of the outcome of the Napoleonic wars. Common Law allows the interpretation from a particular case or situation to be accepted in further situations of the same kind. Common Law has been adopted in most of the countries of the British Commonwealth and in North America, because the early colonists were English and brought over this system of law with them. However, the different states of the United States also have their own laws incorporated within that system.

- Shariah or Islamic Law is based upon the teachings of the Koran and its application to the daily life of the individual. In business matters it particularly applies to such factors as the prohibition of interest on loans.

- Finally, Socialist Law, which affected property rights and the rule of the state upon contracts, was the system applied in the former Communist countries. These countries are rapidly modifying their laws to bring them into line with the market economy they have since adopted.

Most countries have their own particular rules, which are, as mentioned above, an outcome of their history, culture or political system. However, in many cases there are variations and merging. For instance, England, as part of the European Union, has incorporated many aspects of European Law.

In situations where a dispute arises, the parties may find that one law favours the particular problem more than another. For instance, in English contract law there is a requirement, or consideration, for both parties to agree to some form of act that is mutually beneficial to effect the contract. This is to distinguish a contract from a gratuitous promise, or gift. Also, the terms under which a contract is considered invalid, such as *Act of God*, varies with different legal systems. Parties resorting to law in a dispute will therefore wish to resort to a system which favours their particular case.

This is why the law governing the contract should be stated at the outset, in the contract. This will avoid lengthy and costly preliminary investigation as to which law really applies, even before the actual case is heard. It is quite possible, however, for parties from different countries to agree to another law to apply to their contract. For example, a French and an Indian company entering into a contract could agree to Swiss law governing the contract, thus neither party would feel that their partner has undue advantage in case of disagreement. Furthermore, it is quite possible for cases in a foreign legal system to be tried in a different country. That is, the case will be tried in accordance with that country's legal rules.

There is, in effect, an attempt at some sort of international agreement with the uniform laws in the International Sales Act of 1967 which was passed after two corrections at The Hague and was based upon the results of over 30 years. However, there are limitations to this and it is not universally ratified.

Figure 11.1 illustrates the clauses in an international contract.

Figure 11.1 Clauses in an international contract. The complexity of those general terms and clauses indicates the necessity of stating the terms of a contract at the onset in order to avoid costly disputes.

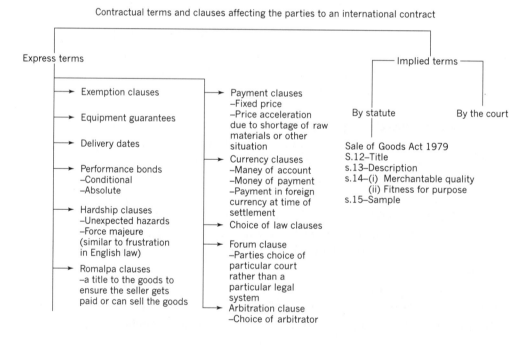

Contractual terms and clauses affecting the parties to an international contract

Express terms

- Exemption clauses
- Equipment guarantees
- Delivery dates
- Performance bonds
  –Conditional
  –Absolute
- Hardship clauses
  –Unexpected hazards
  –Force majeure
  (similar to frustration
  in English law)
- Romalpa clauses
  –a title to the goods to
  ensure the seller gets
  paid or can sell the goods

- Payment clauses
  –Fixed price
  –Price acceleration
  due to shortage of raw
  materials or other
  situation
- Currency clauses
  –Maney of account
  –Money of payment
  –Payment in foreign
  currency at time of
  settlement
- Choice of law clauses
- Forum clause
  –Parties choice of
  particular court
  rather than a
  particular legal
  system
- Arbitration clause
  –Choice of arbitrator

Implied terms

By statute   By the court

Sale of Goods Act 1979
S.12–Title
s.13–Description
s.14–(i) Merchantable quality
     (ii) Fitness for purpose
s.15–Sample

Enforcement

There is, unfortunately, no worldwide authority to enforce laws. Therefore a further problem in international marketing arises, even if a judgement is given in favour of one party, in obtaining redress if the other party resides in another country which has no reciprocal agreement. Some countries have agreed to enforce one another's judgements and the United Nations Commission on International Trade Law (UNCITRAL) is trying to harmonize legal systems, as is the European Union, but despite progress made by those bodies universal agreement does not yet exist.

There are also some reciprocal agreements between individual countries which agree to enforce judgements for one another.

Conventions

In many cases, where certain commercial conditions are found to be mutually desirable by most nations, a number of conventions or agreements by nations participating in the convention have evolved, covering such matters as the CIM convention for the transportation of goods by rail (*Convention Internationale de Maerchandises*) or the Warsaw Convention governing the transportation of goods or passengers by air.

There are many other conventions of a commercial nature, such as the Paris Convention for the protection of industrial property, the Hague Convention for carriage of goods by sea and the New York Convention which binds parties to arbitration awards (see below), as well as many others too numerous to mention. These conventions are yet another step to some form of internationally acceptable set of agreements, though not universal or applicable in all cases.

Arbitration

Another, more informal manner of settling disputes is by way of arbitration. This is when both parties agree to put their case to an independent arbitrator, who need not necessarily be a legal expert but more often a proficient practitioner in a specific commercial area of operations, and therefore well qualified to pronounce a judgement on the case.

This is a popular method of settlement which avoids many of the involved and expensive ways of obtaining redress in a dispute. Arbitrators are usually available from local chambers of commerce or specialist organizations. However, this procedure, while gaining in popularity and legislative advancement in recent years, still suffers from two deficiencies, one being that both parties must agree to this procedure and the other that the party against whom judgement is given may have insufficient assets in the country to cover the award against them.

Conclusions

Altogether this is tricky ground for the marketer and advice should always be obtained on such a specialist issue. The aim here is to alert the student as well as the practitioner to the pitfalls of not stating agreed procedures at the outset and to discuss openly and sincerely areas of mutual concern between trading partners.

Chapter review

Because of differing legal systems all over the world, marketers entering into commercial agreements with foreign trading partners have to decide at the outset which law governs the contract. Failure to do so may mean that there could be an expensive examination process to determine which law applies.

Questions

Section A: Class discussion

1   Why are there so many differing legal systems? State and describe at least two of these.
2   What is meant by the term 'Conflict of Laws' and what are the implications for the international marketer?
3   What are conventions and in what way will they assist international business practice?
4   Why do you think the outcome of a contract could be affected by differing legal systems?
5   Why is arbitration growing in popularity as a method of settling disputes?

Case study

The Black Dart Corporation of Scranton, Ohio, manufacturers of hydraulic lifting gear, have worked since the end of the Second World War with a network of exclusive agents and distributors in continental Europe. Their distributors in Germany are Kornbauer GmbH of Frankfurt who have represented them for many years.

Due to their appreciation of the potential of the German market for their products, Black Dart are considering establishing a subsidiary company in Dusseldorf. This has upset Kornbauer who maintain that this decision breaches their agreement with Black Dart. Black Dart, however, refers to their original agreement, allowable under the laws of the State of Ohio, which consisted of a mutual exchange of letters of intent, automatically renewable until either of the parties opts out.

Kornbauer insist that the success of the company in the German market was due to their diligence and expert salesmanship over the years. They maintain that the original agreement has been superseded by the long-standing working arrangement between the two parties and that the resulting commercial success is mainly due to their input over the years. They threaten to take legal action over this matter.

(This is a totally fictitious case made up to illustrate the problems occurring due to differing points of view and legal systems. It is an analogous compound of various situations observed over time.)

Questions

1   What do you think might be the scenario if Kornbauer takes legal action?
2   Should Black Dart ignore this threat on the basis of the original agreement?
3   If the case went to law, under which legal system is it likely that the case will be tried?
4   Should Black Dart decide to enter into a new agreement with Kornbauer, what do you think should be the new terms to be agreed?

Section B: Examination revision

1 How does history and culture affect the framing of a legal system? Give at least two examples.
2 What are some of the drawbacks of going to arbitration?
3 Which countries, in the main, use Civil Code Law and Common Law, and what are the reasons for this difference?
4 Should parties from different countries wishing to enter into a joint business venture give up the idea because they do not approve of one another's legal system? What are the possibilities open to them?
5 What effect has the European Union upon the English legal system?

References

Phillips, C., Doole, I. and Lowe, R. (1994) *International Marketing Strategy*, International Thomson Business Press, Chapter 12.
Schmitthoff, S. (1990) *The Export Trade*, 9th edn, Stevens & Co.

12

Technical aspects of international marketing

❑ CHAPTER PREVIEW

This is probably the most diverse chapter in the entire textbook. It attempts to give some idea of the complexities of the technical aspects of international marketing. Yet whole books have been written on just one topic within this chapter, such as shipping. So this is just an introduction to the topic. No international marketing manager could be expected to understand all the aspects referred to in this chapter. What one must be aware of is the fact that special expertise in these fields can give an edge over competitors. On the other hand, mistakes in this area can easily lead to disaster.

> A revolution has taken place in international marketing. Small agricultural firms in East Africa are now receiving orders from supermarkets in the UK by e-mail
> *Headline in British newspaper, March 1996.*

This headline epitomizes the revolution which has taken place and is taking place in technical aspects of international marketing, which have changed dramatically over the past 20 years.

This chapter relates to almost all aspects of international marketing, but particularly to long-term planning and commitment.

Without this, an organization will encounter considerable problems in many areas.

❏ BY THE END OF THIS CHAPTER YOU SHOULD:

■ **Understand the significance of technical aspects of international marketing in general**

■ **Be aware of the importance of packing and packaging**

■ **Be aware of the importance of credit insurance**

■ **Understand why the appropriate form of payment for each transaction is essential**

■ **Understand the role of languages in international marketing**

■ **Be aware of the impact of cheaper air fares for passengers, containerization and ro-ro on international marketing**

■ **Be aware of the extreme importance of accurate documentation in international marketing**

■ **Be aware of new technologies such as e-mail and video conferencing in international marketing.** ❏

What are the technical aspects of international marketing?

The technical aspects of international marketing are those aspects which have no direct connection in general with domestic marketing. These include shipping, the use of foreign languages, insurance and terms of payment. Some areas treated in this chapter do appear in domestic marketing, such as shipping and insurance. However, in international marketing they take on a much more important role. Shipping, for the purposes of international marketing, means transport of any kind – rail, air, sea or road. This is, of course, used in the domestic market to transport goods to the customer. The significant difference here is that a mistake in the dispatch of goods to a customer within the home country can usually be put right within a few days. However, in international marketing, if goods are inadvertently shipped to the wrong country, not only will the delay be much longer, but in addition, all kinds of problems can and do occur:

- The documentation will almost certainly be incorrect for the country the goods actually go to. The result will be that the goods will be held up at customs while things are sorted out.
- In the meantime, the customer is waiting for his goods. If he does not receive them on time, perhaps the assembly line will grind to a halt, which will often mean a severe cash penalty for the supplier.
- In the case of seasonal goods, Christmas may be missed, and the buyer may have no use for them.
- Obviously the situation is more serious when the goods are customized, and cannot be replaced out of stock, in order to be sent to the correct destination.

The result of a seemingly slight error may mean not only the loss of an order, but also the loss of a customer, in a world where the competition is fierce.

The main technical aspects of international marketing are containerization, shipping, documentation, changes in shipping design and construction, the use of foreign languages, credit insurance and foreign exchange contracts. We can only examine these areas briefly, but you will find references for further reading at the end of the chapter.

Shipping

This simply means getting the goods to the customer, and today many goods are sent by air rather than by sea. The mode of transport depends on many factors, the ratio of value to weight being one of the most important. Bulk paper of the standard variety is so heavy, compared with its value, that it is impossible to export it profitably even by sea over large distances. With specialized, more valuable papers such as industrial paper filters the situation is different. Two other considerations when considering whether to transport by sea or air freight are speed and security.

Speed

Goods which may be not of high value in themselves may need to be shipped urgently. There may be a sudden demand for a particular model of vehicle or machine, so suddenly extra components are needed over and above the number held in stock. In addition it should be remembered that thanks to Japanese methods of 'just in time', minimum stocks are normally held today. Such urgent orders will normally be sent by air freight. In special circumstances a special plane may have to be chartered, which will cost less than paying penalties for stopping the assembly line, and also hopefully retain the confidence of the customer. Moreover, valuable goods with a low weight to value ratio are routinely sent by air.

Security

Security at airports is usually much stricter than at ports, so goods or cargo which is highly valuable, especially if being shipped to Middle or Far East destinations, is sent by air. Because of the high pilfering rate in some of the world's ports, the extra-high insurance premiums could make it more expensive to send certain goods by sea.

In addition to factors of speed and security, one of the shipping manager's many tasks is to be very familiar with the best routes to choose for the goods to arrive at their destination more quickly and cheaply than the competitor's goods. That way the exporter may save a lot of money which will be reflected in either a lower price charged by him, or a larger profit made on the transaction.

Packing

Packing has three main aspects: security, cost effectiveness and knowledge of the relevant regulations for different countries.

Security

This includes ensuring the goods are packed in such a way that they are unlikely to be damaged on a long sea journey, or even a short flight. Have you ever wondered just how your suitcase could sustain so much damage on a short flight? Perhaps the answer may be in the newer baggage handling machines installed at airports. Goods sent by freight have similar problems, so they must be very well packed. Special packers exist – firms which specialize in packing the goods of small exporters. In addition, in the case of high value goods it means packing and sealing them in such a way that it is immediately obvious on receipt if the goods have been tampered with *en route*.

Cost effectiveness

The experienced shipping manager will know the best method of packing goods so that as many as possible, without packing them too tightly and risking damage, can be stored in one container. This is particularly important with irregularly shaped goods which are not easily stowed, or goods such as chairs or tables which may take up a lot of air space in the container if not properly packed into it. Some goods are designed especially so as to fit more units into a container, and so make shipment much cheaper.

Special regulations

Today many countries have special regulations concerning the packing materials that may be used in goods. Countries such as Sweden and Germany which are highly ecologically conscious ban the use of certain plastic packing materials which are not biodegradable and which could cause poisonous fumes, if put into the furnaces used for disposing of much of the rubbish in those countries. Again, some countries such as New Zealand have very strict regulations as to what kinds of wood may be used in the packing of imported goods. This is because they wish to avoid any kind of timber disease getting into their country. Once established, timber diseases can spread rapidly through a whole country.

Packaging

Legal requirements

Packaging is quite different from the concept of packing although both do refer to the wrapping of goods. Frequently different packaging is required for different countries. This may be for legal reasons. Labelling laws differ from country to country. Products classified as drugs in one country may be classified as a food in another country and as a medicine in a third country. Since all products need to be cleared for entry into a country, the marketing company carries out research as to the labelling requirements for that particular product. Again, in some countries such as Belgium, all labelling must be carried out in two languages. In some countries certain products require instructions for use, but not in others. The ecological factor is important here too. Some countries such as Denmark do not today accept plastic 'bottles'.

Customer expectations

In some countries customers may expect very modest wrapping of the product. In others they expect it to be gift wrapped. If we do not consider the wishes of our customers, we need not be surprised if they buy elsewhere.

Cultural or other differences

The colour, type of font used in labelling and the style of presentation can play just as important a role in selling a product as the advertising for it. This is particularly true of items in supermarkets. In the frequent absence of staff to help with questions, the packet must often sell itself. This applies also to DIY stores and products, where customers need to have the instructions as to how to use it on the packet in certain countries, before they will buy the product.

Methods of payment

This is perhaps the most critical area of technical aspects of international marketing, since without payment for the goods, a firm not only makes no profits, but can very easily become bankrupt, especially if it is a question of an order of a large value. Recovering debts internationally is very difficult and very costly in terms of time and money. So the international marketer is keen to use the appropriate method of payment for each customer.

In international marketing very many of the transactions involved are not one-off opportunities between marketers and customers who will never meet again. On the contrary, since much international business is transacted between organizations which have ongoing needs, a large percentage of international marketing consists of ongoing business between two firms. These could be a shoe manufacturer in Taiwan and a shoe wholesaler based in the United Kingdom. It is evident that once two such firms have entered into an alliance, they will probably wish to continue to do business with each other over a number of years. The buyer in such cases needs the marketer as much as the marketer needs the buyer. Once a sound business relationship has been developed, mutual trust will stem from this, and methods of payment may easily become credit transfer. However, two things must be borne in mind by the supplier:

- How easily in any part of the world a firm, completely creditworthy one day, may be bankrupt the next. There are not always warning signs in advance.
- The larger the volume of business involved, the more prudent both parties may be: if one buyer is accounting for too large a percentage of one's turnover this is good and bad news at the same time; good news because it creates economies in marketing; bad news because if a customer who accounts for 25% of our turnover collapses, then we as suppliers are in serious trouble. Buyers have a similar problem if a firm of suppliers collapses, especially if they cannot easily find another supplier for the product in question.

The experienced international marketer usually knows which methods of payment to offer without upsetting the potential customer, but at the same time being reasonably certain of receiving payment for the goods. When dealing with a new customer from a distant part of the world, who has placed a very large order, prudence dictates that we ask for a form of payment which gives us, the marketer, the best possible chance of being paid for the goods. This method is known as documentary credit, and the form we will discuss now is a confirmed and irrevocable letter of credit. If suppliers have the necessary expertise and experience in this field, they will be virtually certain of being paid for their goods.

How a confirmed and irrevocable letter of credit works

The customer determines what his exact needs are in terms of the order, often having obtained a pro-forma invoice in advance from the supplier of the goods. He then draws up, in consultation with his bank in his country, a letter of credit. This is then sent to the supplier via his bank in his own country. The stipulations of a letter of credit must be observed precisely. If they are not, the bank is not allowed to release payment for the goods. The letter of credit will normally contain the description of the goods and the quantity ordered, along with the price, the way they are to be packed, and the packages and how they are to be labelled. It may also stipulate other conditions such as routing and who insures the goods. It is vital for the supplier to note carefully the contents of the letter of credit immediately it is received, and to verify immediately if he can meet the requirements, e.g. are the goods certain to be ready for shipment in good time? If the supplier has any doubts, he must contact the

Figure 12.1 Procedure for a confirmed irrevocable letter of credit

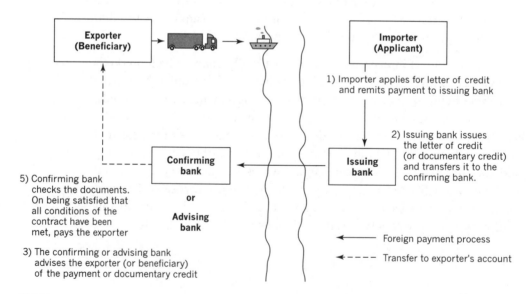

4) Exporter despatches the goods and sends
   the shipment documents to the confirming bank

Exporter (Beneficiary)

Importer (Applicant)

1) Importer applies for letter of credit
   and remits payment to issuing bank

2) Issuing bank issues
   the letter of credit
   (or documentary credit)
   and transfers it to the
   confirming bank.

Confirming bank

or

Advising bank

Issuing bank

5) Confirming bank
   checks the documents.
   On being satisfied that
   all conditions of the
   contract have been
   met, pays the exporter

3) The confirming or advising bank
   advises the exporter (or beneficiary)
   of the payment or documentary credit

———— Foreign payment process

– – – – Transfer to exporter's account

buyer at once by phone or fax and request an amendment of the letter of credit, if that is what is required.

Therefore, we need to make sure in advance that we are going to receive payment for the goods once they are shipped, by using a letter of credit. However, these can be notoriously complicated, and mistakes in this area can be very costly, because once the ship has sailed there may not be another appropriate vessel sailing to that port for another month or more. This can lead to complications because the letter of credit may well have expired in the meantime. Thus expertise is vital in this area. So, firms which need letters of credit have to plan to have the necessary staff trained or recruited to deal with these. The procedures involved are illustrated in Figures 12.1 and 12.2.

Figure 12.2 Procedure for bills of exchange

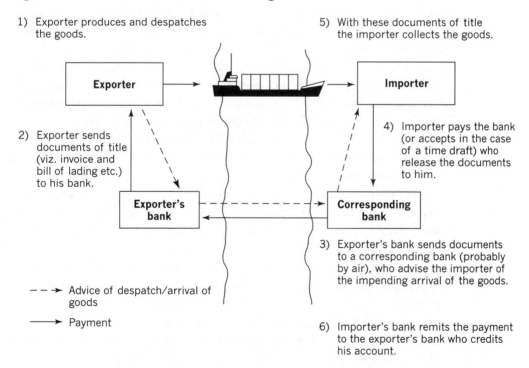

1) Exporter produces and despatches the goods.

5) With these documents of title the importer collects the goods.

2) Exporter sends documents of title (viz. invoice and bill of lading etc.) to his bank.

4) Importer pays the bank (or accepts in the case of a time draft) who release the documents to him.

3) Exporter's bank sends documents to a corresponding bank (probably by air), who advise the importer of the impending arrival of the goods.

– – ► Advice of despatch/arrival of goods

——► Payment

6) Importer's bank remits the payment to the exporter's bank who credits his account.

The use of foreign languages

Much has been written about this subject, and many of the reports particularly point the finger at English-speaking countries. Research shows that many millions of pounds of business are lost to the UK, for example, because so few of its international marketing executives are fluent in foreign languages. True, English is an international language, but if you really want to succeed, you need to speak the language of the buyer – fluently. By this we mean you need to be able to negotiate in the language. If your Swahili or Dutch is only of the basic variety, that doesn't matter so much. The Dutch and Africans use English as an international language and about 80% of Dutch nationals speak English fairly fluently. However, if two executives from different countries meet, one of them must be the master of the other's tongue in order for things to go smoothly, or else use a third language, which is often English.

Interpreters are unsatisfactory most of the time, because you cannot establish social rapport, and also you don't always know what is really happening – what the members of the other team are saying to each other. This is obviously a big drawback in negotiations. The other advantage of having a fluent linguist on your team is that he, or more likely she, will understand the culture of the other side. Cultural differences can be so great, even between neighbouring countries, that important business deals can be blown by a lack of understanding. All international marketers have heard stories such as the British manager inviting his potential French buyer out to lunch and committing the gaffe of taking him to a fast food outlet. Most of the French like to eat a leisurely meal in a quiet atmosphere with delicious well-cooked food, usually with French cuisine.

In some phases of negotiations where teams are involved, and therefore interpreters are being used, it may well be to your advantage to 'hide' your linguist. He or she can then understand what the other team are saying to each other.

Yet, while firms work together very closely internationally, don't forget that in business, as in a game, there is usually only one winner. Therefore maximum effort and skills are needed.

Countries which generally have an excellent track record in international marketing, such as Sweden and Germany, often have executives who speak a number of languages and can therefore gain a rapid rapport with the buyer. The salesperson not only represents the firm for the buyer, he *is* the firm. So, a German buyer will argue, what kind of British firm sends out an executive to do business in Germany, without a word of German? True, there are some industries, such as the computer industry, where English is widely used, but more often the lack of a foreign language is due to the want of a will to learn it.

Documentation

When goods are shipped from one country to another, many documents need to be created. These will typically be a set of invoices, insurance documents and other documents for export and import authorities. If any of the documents is not in order, the implications may be disastrous. It is therefore essential that all staff dealing with export documentation are fully trained in all procedures. In addition, they need to be supervised for some weeks until management is confident that they are likely to be able to perform their tasks with a minimum of errors. They also need to understand the importance of turning to a senior colleague when in doubt. In international marketing, mistakes in documentation often have serious consequences.

The significant reduction in transport and freight costs

If today you are able to buy so many goods produced in distant corners of the earth at affordable prices, this is in part because of the huge reductions in shipping, air freight and air travel costs. Containerization and special purpose-built ships' roll on, roll off techniques, and of course fierce competition between world shipping lines, many of which have disappeared due to the competition of air freight, have all contributed to the revolution and of course to the reduction in transport costs.

INCOTERMS

When a contract is drawn up between buyer and seller, they decide who is going to pay for the freight and insurance costs. This part of the conditions of sale is known worldwide as 'INCOTERMS' (Figure 12.3). We have already examined these under pricing in Chapter 10, so you should refer to that chapter for information on INCOTERMS.

Figure 12.3 New INCOTERMS 1990 – to accommodate multi-model transport

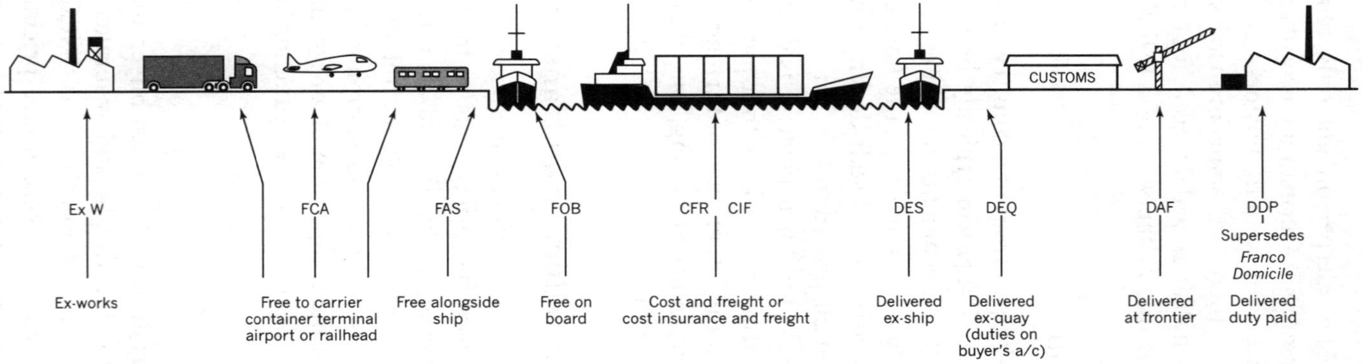

Terms of payment

Within a country, determining terms of payment does not usually call for any expertise. However, in an international marketing context the situation is quite different. It is important to understand the current credit rating of your customer.

The role of the shipper

'Shipper' has two very different meanings in international marketing. It can mean the organization which has manufactured the goods and is exporting them. It can also mean a firm of shippers. Their job is to make sure that the goods are delivered to the appropriate ship or aeroplane. The shippers are experts in logistics and in many cases they deal with much of the documentation of the goods or at least check it to make sure it is in order. See Figures 12.4 and 12.5.

The following true story illustrates how important the technical aspects of international marketing are and how the best of plans can come adrift if the shipping manager is not in control.

Figure 12.4 Demonstration of insurance principles as they affect an exporter's claims for loss or damage to a consignment

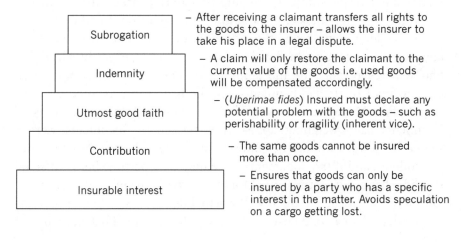

Figure 12.5 Diagram showing the valuation by shippers of cargo freight rates

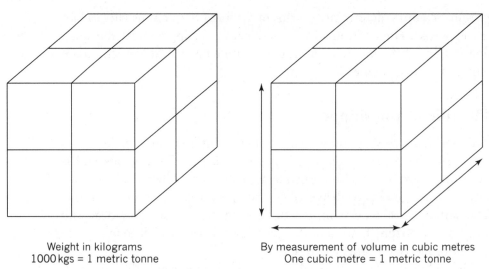

Weight in kilograms
1000 kgs = 1 metric tonne

By measurement of volume in cubic metres
One cubic metre = 1 metric tonne

Weight or measurement
Shippers will choose the higher metric tonnage

The Christmas break

It was five o'clock on Christmas Eve in 1994 and Colette, a shipping manager working in Rugby, England, was about to leave the office. Her firm of shippers had its office inside a multinational company, for which it carried out all the shipping. 'Should I try to ring Bruce one last time?', she wondered. But she knew it would be a waste of time, and that Bruce would be long gone from the office. Bruce did not share Colette's ambition and attention to detail. Bruce was the manager at Heathrow who was responsible for the shipping of one of the most important assignments Colette had handled since she had been promoted to Shipping Office Manager. The consignment consisted of two cartons of documents each weighing about 30 kilos. These documents were a tender for a very important contract in Ankara, Turkey, worth about £40 million, and if the documents were delivered on time her firm stood a good chance of getting it. Moreover, this was just a preliminary contract. The main contract was worth billions, but whoever got the first contract had a good chance of getting the second. That was why the delivery of this consignment to Ankara, before the deadline of Thursday 30 December, was absolutely essential.

This was not the first time Colette had had such a problem. She realized that many countries in the world did not work to Christian holidays, because she dealt with them. She realized, for example, that it was no use phoning most shipping firms in Saudi Arabia on a Friday. That was their main day off, and the day many Moslems went to the mosque.

It is similar for Christmas. While many European countries take a long break and the UK comes to a virtual standstill between Christmas and the New Year, in many countries it is business as usual. The multinational concerned specializes in capital goods, a large percentage of which go to Middle Eastern countries.

Christmas Day was on a Saturday, but Colette was in her office on the Sunday for a few hours catching up with paperwork. She couldn't contact Bruce, but she was praying that he had ensured that the important consignment had left on Christmas Eve, as he had promised.

After Sam left the office, she called on Colette as arranged and they went out together that evening. She and Colette had been friends since Colette arrived in England in 1989. Sam had worked in international marketing and was now a lecturer, and asked if he could come with her to the office the next day to find out more about shipping. Colette agreed. They got to the office at 11 a.m on Monday. The whole factory was deserted because of the holiday and it would not reopen for another week. The first thing Colette did was to contact the airline at Heathrow to find out if her consignment had left. To her horror it had not. It was fortunate she had taken the advice of her first boss – always monitor your plans to see if they are being carried out.

During most of the year the present situation would present no large problem. Colette would have phoned a courier service, and arranged for someone to fly to Ankara by the next plane, taking the documents as personal luggage. That would be the safest way to make sure that they got there on time. Unfortunately it was now Monday and no offices in the South East of England would be working until the following Monday – so no courier was possible! She herself could not go as she had no valid passport – it was being renewed, and she couldn't think of anybody else. Sam had been reading the paper when she put the question to him. How would he like a trip to Ankara?

By the time they realized there was no other solution it was almost two
o'clock. Would Sam have time to collect his passport and toothbrush
from home and be on time for the only plane that day which took off at
17.00 hours? If it had been a normal working day that would have been
impossible, but there was very little traffic on the motorways because of
the holiday, so he made it just in time to Heathrow. The shippers there
conveyed him with the documents to the check in, and soon he was on
the plane to Turkey.

The consignment arrived safely and the firm won the £40 million
contract. However, but for the planning and control of one shipping
manager, the documents would not have arrived on time, and a very
valuable order would have been lost. Technical aspects of international
marketing are therefore of vital importance because all the work involved
in preparing that mountain of documents would have been wasted if the
documents had missed their deadline.

Chapter review

Many different skills apart from marketing are required in international
marketing, and without them no strategy can succeed. Careful planning
is therefore needed to determine which specific skills will be needed by
an organization, and the appropriate staff recruited and trained for those
jobs. These skills include shipping, insurance, documentation and the
use of languages.

Questions

Section A: Class discussion

1 Name two technical aspects which have revolutionized international
   marketing. Examine how they have done this.
2 'Advances in technologies have reduced the importance of personal
   communications in international marketing.' Discuss.
3 Assess the contribution of recruitment of specialized personnel to the
   success of an organization in international marketing.
4 Why in your opinion is shipping so important in international
   marketing?

5 'Containerization has changed the world more than the telephone.' Discuss.

Section B: Examination revision

1 'Technical aspects have no place in a serious textbook on international marketing.' Discuss.
2 Examine the theory that advances in technology tend to promote globalization.
3 Given the task of appointing an international marketing director, what technical aspects would you expect him to master?
4 Technical aspects of international marketing are a major barrier for small and medium-sized enterprises. Why do you think this is so, and how can they viably solve this problem?
5 Critically assess the influence of the reduction of freight rates and air fares over the past two decades on the expansion of world trade.

References

Branch, A. (1981) *Elements of Shipping*, 5th edn, Chapman and Hall.

Branch, A. (1981) *Export Practice and Management*, 3rd edn, Chapman and Hall.

Walker, A.G. (1995) *International Trade Procedures and Management*, Butterworth-Heinemann.

13

The international marketing of services

❏   CHAPTER PREVIEW

Many kinds of services from personal care to financial services and travel and tourism have greatly expanded in the past decade, particularly in OECD countries. Some of these services are much more easily marketed internationally than others. We will examine why this is so and also some reasons why direct marketing can be particularly appropriate for certain market segments and certain types of services.

   This topic relates most closely to the chapter on product strategy, but direct marketing and planning are also important.

❏   BY THE END OF THIS CHAPTER YOU SHOULD:

■   Understand some of the reasons for the rapid expansion in services over the past decade

■   Understand some of the conventional wisdom concerning the difference between the marketing of services and that of products

- Understand the very different characteristics of different services from an international marketing viewpoint
- Understand the significance of direct marketing for some services
- Understand some solutions to traditional problems in the marketing of services.   ❏

Rapid expansion and change of image of certain services

Few sectors of marketing have blossomed as much in the past few years on the domestic scene as the marketing of services, whether it be tourism, banking or insurance. In the case of some services this has meant sheer expansion, in others such as banking and financial services this has led, partly through fiercer competition, to a dramatic change in emphasis in the services offered and also in how they are marketed. Customer care in particular is a concept which has come into the foreground. However, despite the rise in the use and marketing of services, in many cases the international marketing of services is still in its infancy. In other cases the consumer marketing situation is quite different from the business-to-business situation. Bankers' banking is widely international, but few people have a private account with a foreign bank even within their own country. In the travel industry glaring anomalies still exist: according to a report published in September 1997 by the Consumer Association of the UK, some national European airlines, while insisting that they have an international marketing policy, are still clinging to monopolies on specific routes. This enables them to continue, for the time being, to make high profits at the consumers' expense. But the European Commissioners for Competition and for Transport are likely to intervene in the near future.

Two service industries which have become much more international in recent years are the insurance and hotel industries, but in very different ways and for different reasons. There are today a number of hotel chains which have outlets in many countries. This could be arguably to increase customer satisfaction among international travellers, in providing both a uniform standard of service and a comprehensive booking system. The insurance world, on the other hand, has become more international through takeovers, and in many cases the firm doing the takeover has retained the name of the insurance company it has taken over, so as to retain its national identity.

Research forecasts a steady expansion in the UK travel market, as the

Research forecasts steady expansion for UK market

The value of the UK business travel market will continue to grow steadily over the next four years but at a slower rate, according to research by MarketLine International.

The international research company forecast that the value of business travel will grow from £22.8bn in 1997 to £26.5bn in 2001.

But the rate of growth will fall slightly each year, from 4.6% between 1997 and 1998 to 3.5% between 2000 and 2001.

MarketLine analyst Amar Atwal said: "The overall prospects for the UK business travel industry are good, with increases expected in the amount of travellers and their levels of expenditure."

He said growth was due to economic improvement, particularly in trading abroad. This has led to UK companies increasing business and international travel.

But Atwal said at the same time, transport costs are set to fall due to increased competition.

The liberalisation of Europe's skies in April and the development of low-cost carriers were both identified as major contributing factors.

"UK and European airlines are likely to provide a low-cost service similar to that provided by US carriers for passengers travelling from city to city, although effects of the deregulation will be far more gradual in the European Union than in the US where, in the late 70s, fares plummeted and there was an emergence of low-cost carriers," said Atwal.

The report also cited Eurostar as a third factor because it has introduced more competitive pricing with airlines on key routes.

Despite continual growth in business travel expenditure, the UK has not yet returned to the levels of the 80s before the recession of the early 90s.

Levels of expenditure fell 12% between 1989 and 1992.

Source: Travel Weekly, 13 August 1997

article from *Travel Weekly* shows. This trend is reflected in most OECD countries. This upsurge in the marketing of services, and travel in particular, has been led by a number of factors, but particularly increased affluence in many Western countries, more leisure time for many individuals, and an increased popularity of leisure activities, partly a result of the first two factors, but also because the retired segment of Western society has grown due to greater longevity in general. While Third World countries have not experienced this revolution in services, travel and tourism to Third World countries have greatly developed. However, since the tour operators are in many cases based in Western countries, in some cases the cash benefit to the Third World country has been marginal while the effect of tourism itself has had a negative effect on the local culture. One example of this is the effect of tourism on the native North Americans in Canada.

Many OECD countries have witnessed a revolution in the way these services are marketed, and great changes in many countries' legislation permit and encourage this trend. However, this growth has not been matched in every case in the international marketing of services. This is because some services are more difficult to market internationally. This includes such personal services as hairdressing. However, some services such as hotels and air travel have witnessed great success internationally, particularly where business travel and hospitality are concerned. Stressed executives like to know that they are going to receive a familiar pattern of hospitality in different countries. Hence the success of international hotels such as Hilton and Novotel, which are really brand names.

Many factors have accelerated the flow of goods and products from one nation to another, both consumer goods and industrial products, over the past two decades. The growth rate in many OECD countries and the ever-growing demand from customers for increasing international choice are but two of these. Research shows that in the economies of very many developed countries, the value of services produced in the past two decades has been growing much faster in relation to the value of manufactured goods.

Different groups of services

Services can be divided into three groups:

- Personal: medical, hairdressing, beauticians
- Leisure: travel tourism, hobbies, reading
- Financial: banking, insurance, building societies

The marketing of services has been traditionally characterized by the following attributes:

- Intangibility
- Perishability
- Difficulty in providing consistent service
- Simultaneous production and delivery of service

Because of these factors, excellent communications are even more important in the marketing of services than in the marketing of tangible products.

One of the main themes of international marketing during the past decade has been attempts by organizations to use new kinds of marketing, in order to improve their performance. Among these are:

- Direct marketing
- The reduction of intermediaries or middlemen
- Multi-level marketing

Direct marketing

One of the main ideas behind this is that by more specialized segmentation and targeting, a greater percentage of sales can be recorded and hence higher profit margins. If old-fashioned marketing used the shotgun technique, then this uses the sniper method: aim directly at your potential customers. This technique uses modern technologies which were not available to the same extent a decade ago. It especially uses databases, which contain lists of potential customers who are more likely to wish to purchase the particular service or product. These techniques are by no means peculiar to the marketing of services. They are also used to market a large range of products, especially using catalogues which are sent by mail direct to potential customers. One example of this is the marketing of up-market grandfather clocks. This is done using databases of potential customers who have a high disposable income and who have bought similar items in the past. However, it is in the marketing of services that we have seen the greatest increase in the use of direct marketing as tour operators and banks try to reduce costs and cut prices. The following Case study from *Travel Weekly*, 20 August 1997, is an example of this.

Case study: Direct marketing

Direct Holidays looks to agent-bypass plan

Direct Holidays has unveiled plans to bypass travel agents in an attempt to cut cruise prices by up to 50% with the launch of its direct-sell cruise company Direct Cruises.

The company has chartered the 1,434-passenger *Edinburgh Castle* from owner Lowline for itineraries between April and October 1998, cruises depart from Liverpool and Greenock.

The deal is for three years and gives Direct Cruises an option to charter the ship for a further two years.

Direct Holidays chairman John Boyle said the firm offers lower prices because it will not have to pay agents' commission, which he claims can be up to 25% of the total price.

Direct Cruises director Duncan Wilson said the new cruises would fill the gap left by P&O's *Canberra*, which retires from service next month, and CTC's *Southern Cross*, which has been sold to Festival Cruises.

"There is an increased demand and a diminishing supply," he said. "We knew that if we could find a vessel superior to *Canberra* that we could sell at prices at or below those of CTC's, which enabled us to offer a service to match P&O's *Victoria* then we'd have a winner."

Direct Cruises quotes £499 for a 14-night Atlantic Islands cruise, compared to £1,128 for a similar itinerary on Fred Olsen's vessel, *Black Prince*.

A 14-night Mediterranean cruise on *Edinburgh Castle* in August 1998 will cost £1,199, a similar cruise this August on *Canberra* costs £2,885.

Direct Cruises' 1998 brochure has a lead-in price of £399 for a seven-night Norwegian cruise.

Fred Olsen marketing director Nigel Lingard said Direct Cruises were unlikely to harm his business.

"We don't expect that the type of product will be a comparable one," he said. "Taking into account discounts, the differential will not be that great, and what extra price there is to pay will be worth it."

Source: Travel Weekly, 20 August 1997

Air travel

While air travel in general has witnessed a boom period over the past 25 years, there have been dramatic hiccups during this period. The first was caused by the world oil crisis in 1974, when the price of crude oil quadrupled, as a result of the Yom Kippur war in the Middle East. The second was even more sudden and more dramatic, and a result of the invasion of Kuwait by Saddam Hussein of Iraq on 2 August 1990, which led to the Gulf War. As a consequence, tourists from some countries simply stopped travelling abroad, flying in particular. Since perishability is one of the major characteristics of the marketing of services, this means that plane seats not sold before take-off will not be sold at all. It is therefore not surprising that the prices of seats on aeroplanes next to each other could differ by 50% depending on when or how they were sold. Apex tickets sold two weeks in advance can be much cheaper, while standby tickets sold at the last minute can also be much cheaper.

But let us turn to some of the perennial problems of the airline business. One of the main ones is that it is a seasonal business. Most people's holidays are limited to certain times of the year. This can lead to congestion on roads, railways and at airports. Some countries such as Germany have ways of trying to alleviate this problem. In Germany school holidays vary from region to region and are on a rotation basis in order to avoid congestion on motorways and at airports. As a result, there is not the same simultaneous demand for air travel and motorway space as in neighbouring countries.

However, in most countries the result of our pattern of holidays is that airlines have spare capacity during most of the year, and peak times which account for airports being highly congested, airlines stretched to the limits of their capacity, and passengers frequently left delayed and fuming. This is because if they miss one landing or take-off slot they may have to wait some time for another. Worse still, if their aircraft develops a fault it will be unlikely they can find a spare aircraft and the delay can be very long indeed. The passengers incidentally are paying extra for the privilege of flying at these peak times. Is it any wonder that many passengers are tense, nervous and in general difficult to deal with?

Gatwick, Saturday 23 May 1997. Passengers delayed for more than 24 hours due to plane mechanical faults. This nearly caused a riot as unhappy passengers, angered at the delay and lack of information about what was happening, turned aggressive, and the police had to be called in.

While the EU has in general been successful in enforcing the ideas of the Single European Act, air travel is one area where it has so far not promoted the free flow of services, or indeed helped the European traveller. Too many countries have been permitted to continue to subsidize their inefficient national airlines, without being challenged by the European Commission for Competition. As a result many air fares within the EU are disproportionately expensive, due to lack of competition on certain routes. One example: until very recently the return air fare London to Stockholm was considerably more expensive than the return fare London to New York, because of the cartel on the former route by national airlines.

On the other hand, within certain countries, such as the USA and the UK where in general deregulation has been encouraged by legislation, small airlines such as Easyjet are starting to appear. This new breed of airline is offering a no-frills service at cut-price rates. Their characteristics tend to be eliminating the middleman, in this case the travel agent. You book by phoning the airline direct. You are issued a simplified ticket, which cuts down on labour costs. Often, especially on short flights, you may not be served any refreshments at all. The result can be fare reductions in the region of 40% compared with companies offering the traditional services.

Branding

We examined branding briefly in Chapter 8, but we are now going to examine this concept in greater depth since branding in many sectors has taken on much deeper significance over the past two decades. More and more organizations in the service industries are attaching increasing importance to branding. This means they are investing heavily in advertising their name, so that you will remember it, particularly when you take the buying decision.

One reason for this increase in branding is the increase in competition for the customer, who is often bewildered by the choice of possibilities. Very often the familiar name will be chosen because the perception is that it can be trusted. Not only are services partially intangible, they also offer a high risk factor. Once you book in at a hotel, you are at their mercy. Your happiness during your stay there depends on the quality of the facilities and the quality of the services provided. Who has never stayed at a hotel where the bedroom was either over- or underheated and all attempts to change it have failed? Meals and room service can also be major problems for hotel guests. The brand name is designed to put your mind at rest in advance. Here you are guaranteed the ultimate in service! That is the message of the brand name.

Customer loyalty schemes

This increase in emphasis on branding is also linked to customer loyalty, and the concept that it costs 6–30 times more to gain a new customer than to keep a current one. This is one reason why there has been such an emphasis on customer loyalty during the past decade. This takes many different forms and includes:

- Special offers to current customers
- Reward or loyalty cards used by supermarkets, airlines and hotels
- 'Club membership' of theatres and leisure centres, which offer discounts of up to 50% to regular customers.

These are just some examples. Can you think of some others we have not mentioned?

All of these schemes have similar objectives. They aim to make customers feel wanted in more than one way. Customers feel special because the company writes to them with special offers which the general public do not always receive. As well as reductions in price they can often book early for theatre seats, thus getting first choice. Customer loyalty has some common factors with branding and also with direct marketing. Both rely on relatively new techniques of using databases to keep records of their customers' profiles and tastes.

Branding was originally used mainly with tangible products, and we will examine briefly why it became so important for so many companies, before it came to be heavily used in the marketing of services.

The international branding of services

Despite huge increases in the spend on the marketing of services, the internationalization of this sector remains very patchy. This is partly because of different legislation in different countries, especially in sectors such as banking. In addition, customers' perception of certain industries is such that they would not want to bank with a foreign company. They may perceive the risk to be too great, even if the interest rates are more advantageous.

Chapter review

The use of and profile of services have been on the increase in the past two decades. Competition has greatly increased and as each company strives to increase its share of the market, more and more are turning to branding and loyalty schemes as the solution to their problems.

Questions

Section A: Class discussion

1 List some of the traditional characteristics of the marketing of services.
2 Critically examine the concepts of heterogeneity and perishability and analyse some of their implications.
3 Describe some of the more practical differences in the delivery of services and that of products.
4 Is uniformity in the delivery of a service always desirable?
5 Which services are the most difficult to market internationally?

Section B: Examination revision

1 Discuss the opinion that there is really very little difference between the marketing of services and the marketing of products.
2 Can you see a connection between direct marketing and the marketing of services?
3 Do you consider that different services need to be marketed differently internationally?

4   Describe how European Union directives have affected the marketing of services within that area.

5   Give an example of a service which has had to change its marketing focus.

14

SMEs and two important world markets

CHAPTER PREVIEW

Many textbooks on international marketing concentrate on larger firms and especially on MNCs, tending to ignore the role of SMEs. While the majority of SMEs are not involved today in international marketing, those that are show some surprising success stories, and it is highly likely in the future that more will need to concern themselves with overseas markets. We will also examine two very important world markets, Germany and Japan, as they represent desirable target markets for many international marketing organizations.

These topics relate to many of the theories which you have already studied throughout this book. While some of the companies quoted in previous chapters have been small or medium-sized enterprises, nearly all firms start off like this.

❏ BY THE END OF THIS CHAPTER YOU SHOULD:

■ Understand the key role of SMEs in international marketing

■ Understand why many SMEs are only partially involved in international marketing or not at all

■ **Understand why government help and help from the private sector towards SMEs is often misdirected and underused**

■ **Be aware of the importance of SMEs for the future**

■ **Understand some reasons for the success of Germany and Japan as international marketing nations**

■ **Understand some of the requirements to succeed in international marketing in Germany and Japan.**   ❑

SMEs – an alien world?

Throughout their career at business school, students study the world of business. Much of their information is obtained from reading newspapers and journals which describe companies and their successes and failures. Newspapers tend to reflect what their readers are interested in, and this interest is almost exclusively in the larger companies. There are at least two reasons for this. The larger companies are much more capable of newsworthy feats – giant takeovers and massive disasters. Again, the national – or even international – public is familiar with the product and wants to know the story behind it. Secondly, much of the information in the financial pages is used to help investors get a better picture of the companies involved and the way they work, so that investment decisions can more easily be taken. Many institutions tend to invest in large stocks rather than in small companies. The newspaper stories therefore concentrate on the larger companies and their shares.

Multinational companies often do not use the tools of international marketing used by the smaller company. This is because many of them are centrally organized. The basic product may be determined by a head office in a distant country. The product may then be shipped to overseas markets, and the manager responsible for that market may have very little say in the adaptation of the product for that market.

However, while in most countries the largest companies account for the major share in value of the country's exports, without the contribution of the smaller companies many of these countries would be showing a balance of trade deficit.

Research on SMEs

Two statements can be made concerning the low profile of SMEs, at least in OECD countries. Firstly, this low profile cannot be attributed to lack of research in this area. Secondly, different research projects carried out in a number of EU countries over three decades tend to come up with similar results. There is, however, to date a lack of literature on the direct comparison of the performance of SMEs in exporting in different countries. However, the authors are currently carrying out research in this area and we hope to have more evidence for our second edition.

Definition of SMEs

One thing SMEs have in common is a lack of homogeneity. Many different definitions are used, varying from a firm with 500 employees to one-man bands. Definitions which concentrate on the size of the firm's turnover are just as varied.

Confederation of British Industry survey on SMEs and international marketing

While there is no lack of research on SMEs and international marketing, much of it tends to come from widely different sources. However, from research undertaken by Tookey 30 years ago up to the most recent research there does seem to be a consensus as to the approach of SMEs to international marketing, and also in the approach which governments take in their attempts to 'help' or 'encourage' SMEs' efforts to become involved in overseas markets.

The results of the SME Council of the Confederation of British Industry, published in 1996 under the title *Trade Secrets*, encapsulate the findings of other researchers in this area. We will therefore quote these findings at some length, as they help to explain the situation found in many SMEs and their difficulties in the area of international marketing.

Why do SMEs become involved in international marketing?

The most quoted reason for SMEs starting off in international marketing was 'Strategic growth potential', followed by 'Greater stability' with

Figure 14.1 Why do companies start exporting?
Source: CBI survey 1996

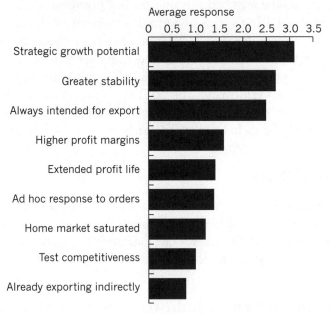

(respondents were asked to score on a scale of 1–4, where 1 is a minor reason
and 4 is a major reason)

'Always intended for export' coming third in importance. The full picture is given in Figure 14.1.

Why do some SMEs not *become involved in international marketing?*

The most cited reason was 'No time to consider', followed by 'Product not suitable' and then 'Entry cost too high'. The full picture is given in Figure 14.2.

How can SMEs be persuaded to become involved in international marketing?

In the past, often the SME needed to know that it would succeed in overseas markets before it would even try. So it was a chicken and egg situation! While successive British governments have talked a lot about

Figure 14.2 What are the main reasons for the decision not to export on a proactive basis?
Source: CBI survey 1996

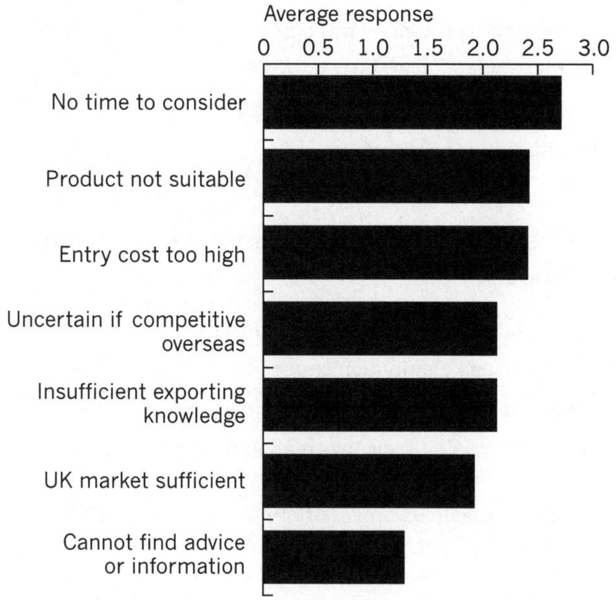

Average response

| | | | | | | |
|0|0.5|1.0|1.5|2.0|2.5|3.0|

No time to consider

Product not suitable

Entry cost too high

Uncertain if competitive overseas

Insufficient exporting knowledge

UK market sufficient

Cannot find advice or information

(respondents were asked to score on a scale of 1–4, where 1 is a minor reason and 4 is a major reason)

helping small firms become involved in overseas markets, the bureaucracy involved has often served to put small firms off. Some years ago, for example, the British government devised a scheme to subsidize market research by small firms in overseas markets. However, the paperwork involved was horrendous, and very few firms even bothered applying for the money.

Many countries have government schemes to help exporters, but industry, especially small firms, complain that many of these are schemes devised by bureaucrats for bureaucrats. They do not correspond to the needs of small firms, and research needs to be done into this area.

Why do SMEs fail in overseas markets?

The main reason seems clear: their failure to appreciate the amount of resources, time and skills needed. It is interesting to compare the results,

Figure 14.3 Reasons for failure of inexperienced exporters
Source: CBI survey 1996

Failure to dedicate sufficient resources	57%
Inability to take a long-term approach	37%
Cultural/language problems	37%
Poor overseas distribution capability	30%
Insufficiently trained people	27%

Figure 14.4 Reasons for failure of experienced exporters
Source: CBI survey 1996

Failure to dedicate sufficient resources	41%
Poor overseas distribution capability	39%
Failure to obtain sufficient market information	29%
Failure to obtain timely information on sales opportunities	20%
Unable to meet customer requirements	20%

given by the firms themselves, of firms with experience in exporting and firms without such experience. While the details are different, resources is at the top of each list (Figures 14.3 and 14.4).

How can experienced SME exporters improve?

● Only 19% invoice in anything other than sterling
● Nearly three-quarters of smaller exporters do not undertake export training

What do they need?

For experienced exporters, the most important ingredient of success was product quality. At this stage, exporting has clearly been integrated into the business plan and success relies on the core business factors of quality, price and speed (Figure 14.5). The special nature of doing business overseas only emerges through the premium placed on personal relationships and distributor quality, both reflecting the risk and communication difficulties associated with long distance ventures. Experienced SME

Figure 14.5 Key factors to export success
Source: CBI survey 1996

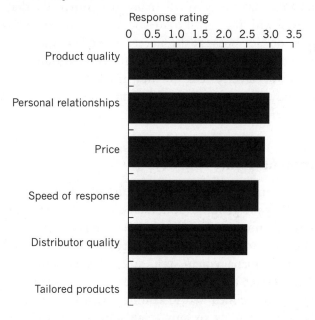

(respondents were asked to score on a scale of 1–4, where 1 is a minor factor
and 4 is a major factor)

exporters are also less concerned about access to advice. Instead, they see the biggest barriers to success as the difficulties they face in identifying suitable overseas representatives and obtaining up-to-date information. Certain sector-specific problems were identified, and while these are not specifically addressed in this report, some – such as the need to provide on-demand bonds – will be the subject of separate CBI work.

Information and advice

The CBI survey found that the experience and usage levels of the services of the Export Development Counsellors, as well as the range of information services, were low within this group of respondents. While awareness levels are high, these companies have either developed their own networks or regard such services as inappropriate to their needs.

Conclusions

The fact remains that many small firms are convinced that they can manage very well with their own domestic market and are aware in many cases that they do not possess the necessary skilled staff for taking on overseas markets. However, with increasing competition from overseas firms, they too will have to seek out new markets.

The case study, Frank Brown of Luton, shows that SMEs can be successful in international marketing.

Specific international markets

It is impossible to understand the true nature of international marketing in a vacuum. To gain genuine understanding you must study specific markets. As we pointed out in Chapter 5 on market selection strategy, one of the most important factors in this area is the fit or match between the organization, its management style, size, products and manufacturing process and the target market. It would be inappropriate, for example, for a firm based in a Third World country with low technical and low quality consumer products to aim at an affluent OECD country as a prime market.

We have chosen two markets to examine briefly to sum up the kinds of characteristics which an international marketer might be looking for in a market. This, however, we repeat depends on the characteristics of the

---

**Helping people think internationally
Frank Brown & Son, Luton**

Helen Brown, Director and Company Secretary

The company, formed in 1966 by Frank and Clive Brown, began operation with one lathe, two milling machines and one customer, growing steadily over the years and moving to our present premises in 1978.

As the years progressed, it became obvious there was a need for a change of direction, to move away from the automotive industry and be prepared to diversify into new areas. Our main effort was one of a continuous directive towards the airline world.

We have now expanded through internal growth to our present size as one of the world's leading designers and manufacturers of aircraft and engine ground support equipment and special tooling. We are the manufacturer of Brenco 'Stepfast' jacks and the authorized UK distributor for 'carr lane' tooling aids and components.

In opening up new markets we rely mainly on our reputation as one of the leading companies in our field, and our name can be seen on stands and tooling at different airports throughout the world. We now manufacture to ninety different airlines, and are the licensed manufacturers for both Rolls-Royce and C.F.M.I. SNECMA aero-engine tooling.

There is a basic requirement for the highest level of quality in our business, and it has always been the company's goal to maintain and improve upon our standards.

We invest continuously in research and development which is, of course, very expensive, but it is absolutely essential to keep abreast of the market and product developments to maintain our present level of quality. We network with the aero manufacturers and the airlines to keep in touch with current trends.

There is a constant need to train and re-train people to keep abreast of new situations and directives. Therefore, in 1989–90 we embarked upon a comprehensive training programme to bring about a total quality approach. This training effort was an important investment for us because as the company grew, we knew we needed to become as professional as possible.

In September, 1990, we became corporate members of the Lifting Equipment Engineers Association, and in November of that year became BS5750 part 1 approved. The following August, we achieved MOD Quality approval AQAP 1.

The company has developed to such an extent that our management team can now maintain the momentum and operate independently within the structure. Supervisors are now responsible to a greater level than they were before and the whole team can carry the professionalism of the company through our expansion and into new markets.

As we've grown in size and scope, so have the workforce, they have all developed and trained their minds to working on an international level. The whole company gets a 'buzz' from making our equipment and seeing it being shipped to various parts of the world, and it is important for us to make the most of this in the interest of the company. The workforce is committed to our aims and we maintain that commitment by treating everyone as an integral and important member of the company. We're all here to produce a specialized product and without each one of us carrying out our own particular job well the cycle would not be complete.

It has been a difficult task for a company of our size and location to become international. What we have achieved has been through sheer hard work and determination on our part. Being a part of the global market does create many problems, there is always a great deal of bureaucracy to untangle and never-ending regulations to work through.

As far as Europe is concerned, we look forward to the arrival of a single set of rules and regulations on materials and standards – without involving reams of documentation and paperwork. A standard VAT rate within the EC would help as well!

To be able to succeed in international business you have to be a particular type of person. You need to be well disciplined and to appreciate and enjoy a real challenge. It can be quite difficult coping with the constant pressure all the time. You have to make a determined effort to get out, knock on doors and sell, sometimes brochures and other promotional material are just not sufficient.

We persisted and I must admit it has been difficult, but I think we can honestly say we have so far been successful in our international endeavours.

Quality accreditation is only part of the process of achieving total quality. Accreditation ought always to lead to a rethink of processes and systems, both in manufacturing and in terms of communication processes in the company. The need to stay ahead of the field means taking seriously the idea of continuous improvement. Active promotion of a flow of ideas and suggestions for change and improvement from all parts of the company, and helping people take real responsibility to act together so that the whole effort of the business is greater than the sum of the parts: these are the keys to securing commitment from all the people in the company in a fast-moving international environment.

firm and its products, and of course its willingness to allocate resources and, if necessary, adapt its product for other markets.

The Federal Republic of Germany

The Federal Republic of Germany is a modern democratic country with a population of over 80 million people, and one of the highest standards of living in the European Union. It is a highly desirable market for many marketers because of the following factors:

- A very high gross domestic product
- A very high gross domestic product per capita
- A sound industrial base built on a number of high technological industries
- Politically stable
- Excellent access to it by air, road, rail and sea
- Excellent communications within the country
- Buyers and consumers are not hostile to foreign-produced goods

The prosperity which Germany built up after the Second World War had a very solid base. Although the country is not rich in mineral wealth, the workforce is highly skilled and motivated. It is therefore a prime market for international marketers.

The recipe for success in the German market

However, to succeed in the German marketplace a firm needs the following:

- Long-term commitment and a plan for working with its potential German partner
- High standards of quality and design
- High levels of commercial and technical competence as discussed in Chapter 3
- Competitive prices
- Awareness of the cultural differences between the regions of the country; this is especially important for firms marketing foodstuffs or drinks.

It is interesting to note that although the United Kingdom believes it is successful in exporting to Germany, in fact Belgium, a country with only a fraction of the inhabitants and GNP, actually exports more to Germany!

Japan

Japan and Germany are two of the leading international marketing countries in the world and have over the past several decades showed a surplus in their balance of payments. Japan's leading role as an industrial nation dates only from after the Second World War.

Japan as an international market

Japan too is a democratic country, with a population of about 120 million people, and a very high standard of living. The factors which make it attractive are very similar to Germany (see above). However, the Japanese have a tendency still to prefer to buy Japanese goods, and this is one of the factors which makes it a difficult market for many Western firms.

Kentucky Fried Chicken – one firm that succeeded in Japan

The story of Kentucky Fried Chicken in Japan is so classical that it doesn't matter that the beginning of the story dates back to 1970. This is because in many ways the secret of successful marketing in Japan by foreign firms remains basically the same – adapt or fail.

Kentucky Fried Chicken noted in 1970 not only that Japan was the second largest consumer market in the world, but also that eating out there represented a turnover of $55 billion per year. Moreover, this figure was growing fast, and rapid expansion of a market often means that above-average profit margins are possible.

Starting from scratch, Kentucky Fried Chicken had a turnover of more than $200 million per annum, within 11 years, through 324 outlets, of which 125 were owned by the organization and 199 were run by franchisees.

In 1970 KFC recruited Loy Weston from IBM to head up their Japanese operations. His recipe for success was radical but simple – adapt to the requirements of the Japanese market. This is something that many foreign firms before and since had not done and as a result had failed in the Japanese market. One of Loy Weston's first steps was to recruit a Japanese executive, who was to take many of the major market-ing decisions of the company. Loy admitted that he did not always understand these decisions. Japanese culture is very different in many ways from US culture, but Loy would reiterate 'This is **Japan!**', mean-ing that in order to succeed in Japan you must do things in the Japanese way. Sometimes this means combining the latest modern technology with ancient Japanese traditions. An example of this is the measures that were necessary when they opened their first store in Japan. Senior KFC executives visited the owners of neighbouring stores, including compe-titors, presenting them with gifts and inviting them to the opening ceremony. During this ceremony there was a combination of Western and Japanese traditions. A Shinto priest held a blessing ceremony many hundreds of years old, while the opening tape was cut with scissors in Western style.

After conducting market research, some changes were made to the menu to accommodate Japanese tastes, and they quickly discovered that the standard US size store would not fit into the smaller dimensions of Japanese city streets.

These are just some examples of the ways in which Kentucky Fried Chicken adapted its marketing, in order to succeed in the Japanese market. The important thing was, they knew they could not simply offer a totally US product in a totally US way in Japan and hope to succeed.

International marketing in the twenty-first century

It is difficult to predict which directions international marketing will take in the next century, and we can be pretty sure only of uncertainty. The rate of change in inventions and the dramatic shortening of time between the beginning of research on a product and the launch of that product in the shops indicates that change due to technology is becoming more and more rapid.

It is because of these many simultaneous changes in the world today that many modern business strategists believe in the chaos theory. The chaos theory attempts to explain why seemingly ordered patterns turn suddenly and unexpectedly into chaos. An example of such an unex-pected event was the crash in Wall Street in 1987 which took experts aback. As world stock markets become more closely linked there exists the danger that a crash in one stock market will bring about a disastrous domino effect which could embrace them all. Again, certain economies like Japan play such a key role in world trade and investment that a deep recession in Japan would almost certainly seriously affect all nations.

While the imbalance in wealth between the richest and poorest countries is likely to change significantly in the next 20 years, certain projections of world population and world trade suggest that certain countries such as Indonesia, Malaysia and China will be playing a much more important role in world trade, and will be markets much more worthy of study than in the past.

One last thought worthwhile considering: in 1995 the World Trade Organization took over the settlement of world trade disputes from GATT, the General Agreement on Tariffs and Trade, which had been performing this function since 1948. It is too soon to tell what difference the new organization will make, but it seems at the time of writing that it is likely to play a different, tougher role than its predecessor, and that it may contribute to changes in the pattern of world trade rather than resist them.

Chapter review

SMEs have different problems with overseas markets than larger firms. We have examined what these are and often it is lack of commitment that has led to their non-involvement with overseas markets and failure in those which have tried. We have also discussed the main reasons Germany and Japan are desirable markets and how to succeed in those markets. Do not look to the past to predict the future.

Questions

Section A: Class discussion

1 Why do many SMEs not seriously consider overseas markets?
2 What do the graphs on pages 213 to 215 tell you about the planning of SMEs?
3 Which information about Germany do you think is more relevant for the marketer of consumer goods and which for the organizational marketer?
4 Why do you think many firms fail in the German market?

5 What do you think is the biggest problem in marketing in Japan for overseas firms?

Section B: Examination revision

1 Do you think that SMEs use the same international marketing methods as MNCs?
2 Do you think that SMEs have the same problems in overseas markets as MNCs?
3 As an international marketing manager, what steps would you take to ensure that your consumer goods were successful in Japan?
4 Discuss some reasons for the international success of German or Japanese firms.
5 Do you think it likely that Germany and Japan will be replaced as the leading industrial and marketing nations in the next 20 years? State your reasons.

References

CBI SME Council (1996) *Trade Secrets.*
Facts about Germany, published by the German Ministry of Information.
Larke, R. (1994) *Japanese Retailing*, Routledge.

MAIN THEMES OF CHAPTER 1

TOSHIBA'S LAUNCH OF LAPTOP COMPUTER

SUCCESS BASED ON:

- INNOVATION
  - IN MARKETING
  - IN OPERATIONS MANAGEMENT
- AWARENESS OF
  - COMPETITION
  - CHANGE

SWATCH'S FACTORS FOR SUCCESS

- EMPHASIS OF 'MADE IN' CONCEPT
- COMBINED WITH ADVANCED DESIGN COLOURS AND APPEAL TO FASHION

SOME GENERAL REASONS FOR INTERNATIONAL MARKETING

- TO IMPROVE PROFITABILITY THROUGH INCREASED SALES
- FINDING PROFITABLE NICHE IN A MARKET
- ECONOMIES OF SCALE
- EXPLOITATION OF A PRODUCT WHICH IS SUITED TO DEVELOPING COUNTRIES

MAIN THEMES OF CHAPTER 2

THE IMPLICATIONS OF LONG-TERM PLANNING
COMMITMENT AND INVESTMENT:

- TWO SECRETS OF CHUPA CHUPS' SUCCESS:
    - EXCELLENCE AT ONE THING
    - SPREADING YOUR RISKS
- CAPITAL NEEDED FOR: MARKET ENTRY STRATEGIES;
  TRAINING IN TECHNICAL ASPECTS; RECRUITMENT OF
  SPECIALIZED PERSONNEL

MARKETING PLANNING
FLEXIBILITY AND ADAPTING TO CHANGE

ORGANIZATIONAL MARKETING IS CRUCIAL FOR INTERNA-
TIONAL MARKETING: FEW CUSTOMERS SO THEY MUST BE
CHERISHED

GLOBALIZATION AND PRODUCT ADAPTATION:
WHEN ARE EACH APPROPRIATE?

EFFECTIVENESS OF SEGMENTATION AND TARGETING

MAIN THEMES OF CHAPTER 3

- IMPORTANT NOT TO TAKE ON TOO MANY MARKETS
- SIGNIFICANCE OF COMMUNICATIONS WITH THE MARKET
- COMPONENTS AND IMPORTANCE OF COMMERCIAL COMPETENCE
- COMPONENTS AND IMPORTANCE OF TECHNICAL COMPETENCE
- IMPORTANCE OF SOCIAL RELATIONS BETWEEN BUYER AND SUPPLIER
- ROLE OF NEGOTIATIONS IN INTERNATIONAL MARKETING
- DIFFERENT APPROACHES TO NEGOTIATIONS CAN ARISE FROM CULTURAL DIFFERENCES
- IMPORTANCE OF BEING AWARE IN ADVANCE OF CULTURAL ATTITUDE OF PARTNERS TO NEGOTIATIONS
- OFTEN THE REASONS FOR FAILURE OF A FIRM IN INTERNATIONAL MARKETING ARE IN ITS OVERALL CULTURE
- ORGANIZATIONS OFTEN EMBARK ON INTERNATIONAL MARKETING WITHOUT SUFFICIENT EXPERTISE

MAIN THEMES OF CHAPTER 4

- CULTURE IS LEARNT FROM THOSE AROUND US
- CULTURE GENERATES ATTITUDES WHICH AFFECT ALL MARKETING OPERATIONS
- CULTURE IS THE OUTCOME OF MANY FACTORS: THE ENVIRONMENT, CLIMATE, GEOGRAPHY, HISTORY, GOVERNMENT, RELIGION
- CULTURE COMPRISES MANY FACTORS SUCH AS:
  - IDEAS, ATTITUDES, VALUES AND SYMBOLS (KEEGAN)
  - ALSO RELIGION, FAMILY INFLUENCE, EDUCATION, LANGUAGE, SOCIAL STRUCTURE AND OTHER ASPECTS
  - CULTURAL ATTITUDES
  - CULTURAL ORIENTATIONS
- FACTORS ARE INTERLINKED AND AFFECTED BY ONE ANOTHER
- ALL AFFECT CIRCUMSTANCES AND OPERATIONS TO DO WITH MARKETING

MAIN THEMES OF CHAPTER 5

- IMPACT OF PLANNING ON MARKET ENTRY STRATEGY
- IMPORTANCE FOR SMES OF PRIORITIZING MARKETS
- ROLE OF INVESTMENT IN MARKET RESEARCH PRIOR TO TAKING MAJOR MARKET ENTRY DECISIONS
- NEED FOR CLEAR OBJECTIVES FOR MARKET RESEARCH
- MARKET ENTRY BARRIERS CAN BE USED AS AN ADVANTAGE
- KNOW-HOW NEEDED IN HOW TO EXPLOIT FREE TRADE ASSOCIATION OPPORTUNITIES

MAIN THEMES OF CHAPTER 6

- PLANNING OF ORGANIZATION FOR MARKET ENTRY STRATEGY
- THE ADVANTAGES OF LICENSING:
    - LESS CAPITAL INVOLVED
    - CAN GAIN ACCESS TO DIFFICULT MARKETS
- ADVANTAGES OF MANUFACTURE OVERSEAS:
    - LOW PRODUCTION COSTS
    - LOW LABOUR COSTS
    - AVOID TARIFFS PAYABLE FOR THE FREE TRADE ASSOCIATION
- CONTRACT MANUFACTURE:
    - LOWER COSTS
    - NO CAPITAL OUTLAY
- COUNTERTRADE:
    - ESSENTIAL TO CONSIDER THIS WHEN DEALING WITH CERTAIN COUNTRIES; HOWEVER, IT CONTAINS PITFALLS

MAIN THEMES OF CHAPTER 7

- ROLES OF EXPORT AND CONFIRMING HOUSES
- USE OF BRANCH OFFICE IN TARGET MARKET
- USE OF OWN MARKETING SUBSIDIARY ABROAD
- ESSENTIAL DIFFERENCES BETWEEN AN AGENT AND A DISTRIBUTOR
- APPOINTING AN AGENT
- APPOINTING A DISTRIBUTOR
- MAIN AIM: CONTROL OF THE MARKETING

MAIN THEMES OF CHAPTER 8

- PRODUCT STRATEGY STARTS WITH SOME PENETRATING QUESTIONS:
  - WHAT BUSINESS ARE WE IN?
  - WHERE IS OUR MARKET AND WHERE IS IT GOING? – WHAT ARE THE TRENDS?
  - WHAT FACTORS INFLUENCE THE MARKET?
  - WHAT MARKETING OBJECTIVES DO WE NEED?
  - WHAT ARE OUR OVERALL MARKETING STRATEGIES?
  - IS THE MARKET CHANGING IN SIZE, STRUCTURE, LOCATION OR NATURE?
  - ARE THERE GAPS IN THE MARKET TO BE EXPLOITED?
  - WHAT ARE THE COMPETITION'S ACTIVITIES AND STRATEGIES?
  - WHAT IS THE CURRENT SEGMENT? DOES IT NEED ADJUSTING?
  - DO WE UNDERSTAND THE CUSTOMERS' NEEDS?
  - IS THERE SUFFICIENT QUANTITATIVE AND QUALITATIVE RESEARCH DATA?
- TOTAL PRODUCT CONCEPT
- GLOBALIZATION
- BRANDING
- MARKET PROFILE ANALYSIS MODEL
- MARKETING MIX AGAINST MARKET CHARACTERISTICS
- ALL ASPECTS OF THE MARKETING MIX INTERRELATED
- EXAMINE EVERY CELL IN THE MODEL

MAIN THEMES OF CHAPTER 9

- MARKET SEGMENTS SUPERIMPOSED WITH REGIONAL FACTORS
- THE COMMUNICATION PROCESS
- ELEMENTS OF THE COMMUNICATION PROCESS
    - SOURCE
    - TARGET MARKET
    - MESSAGE VARIANTS
    - LINGUISTIC
    - CULTURAL
    - LEGAL
    - MEDIA
    - TIMING
- INTERNATIONAL TRADE FAIRS AND EXHIBITIONS
    - AIMS OF AN INTERNATIONAL EXHIBITION
    - PREPARATION FOR AN INTERNATIONAL TRADE FAIR
    - ACTIVITIES DURING THE EXHIBITION
- PERSONAL SELLING

MAIN THEMES OF CHAPTER 10

- SETTING THE PRICE OF A PRODUCT IS AN INTEGRAL PART OF THE MARKETING MIX
- THE SAME PRINCIPLES APPLY IN INTERNATIONAL MARKETING
- MAIN STRATEGIES ARE: SKIMMING, PENETRATION AND COST PLUS, ALSO WHAT THE MARKET WILL BEAR AND FOLLOW THE COMPETITION
- CONDITIONS VARY WITH DIFFERENT MARKETS
- OFTEN COMPANIES USE INTERMEDIARIES SUCH AS AGENTS AND DISTRIBUTORS
- RELIANCE ON THESE INTERMEDIARIES BUT AWARENESS OF DIFFERING OBJECTIVES BETWEEN PRINCIPAL AND INTERMEDIARY
- COST MAKE-UP IN INTERNATIONAL MARKETING
- MARGINAL PRICING – ITS POSSIBILITIES AND PITFALLS
- TRANSFER PRICING BY MNCS AND ITS DANGERS
- TENDER BIDDING PROCEDURES AND PRICING DECISIONS

MAIN THEMES OF CHAPTER 11

- COUNTRIES DEVELOP THEIR LEGAL SYSTEMS ACCORDING TO HISTORICAL, CULTURAL, RELIGIOUS AND POLITICAL BACKGROUNDS
- DIFFERENT LAWS AND LEGAL SYSTEMS MAY LEAD TO DIFFERENT JUDGEMENTS
- PARTIES ENTERING INTO A BUSINESS VENTURE SHOULD DECIDE WHICH LAW APPLIES TO THE CONTRACT
- AN INDEPENDENT LEGAL SYSTEM TO EITHER OF THE PARTIES IS A POSSIBILITY
- THERE ARE A NUMBER OF EXISTING CONVENTIONS AND UNIFORM RULES WHICH MIGHT APPLY
- IF NO SYSTEM IS STATED, THERE WILL BE A PROCESS TO DEDUCE WHICH SYSTEM SHOULD APPLY
- ARBITRATION IS A POPULAR METHOD OF RESOLVING DISPUTES

MAIN THEMES OF CHAPTER 12

- WHAT THE TECHNICAL ASPECTS ARE
- SHIPPING, INSURANCE, DOCUMENTATION
- TERMS OF PAYMENT
- METHODS OF PAYMENT
- LETTERS OF CREDIT
- USE OF LANGUAGES
- IMPORTANCE OF RECRUITING AND/OR TRAINING SUITABLE STAFF

MAIN THEMES OF CHAPTER 13

- INCREASE IN THE USE OF SERVICES AND IN THE COMPETITION IN THAT SECTOR
- DIFFERENT CHARACTERISTICS OF SERVICES:
    - INTANGIBILITY
    - PERISHABILITY
    - PROBLEMS IN PROVIDING A UNIFORM SERVICE
- INCREASED USE OF:
    - DIRECT MARKETING
    - LOYALTY SCHEMES
    - BRANDING
- DIVERSIFIED DEGREE OF INTERNATIONALIZATION OF THE MARKETING OF SERVICES

MAIN THEMES OF CHAPTER 14

- SMES AND THEIR PROBLEMS IN OVERSEAS MARKETS
- LIKELY FUTURE TRENDS OF SMES
- GERMANY: WHY IT IS A DESIRABLE TARGET MARKET
  - WHAT YOU NEED TO DO TO SUCCEED THERE
- JAPAN AS A TARGET MARKET
  - PROBLEMS OF THE JAPANESE MARKET
  - KENTUCKY FRIED CHICKEN IN JAPAN
  - HOW KFC OVERCAME THE PROBLEMS OF JAPANESE CULTURE

Index